Tennis For the Rest of Us

A Practical Guide for the New, Nearly New,
Newly Frustrated, or Nearly Discouraged Tennis Player

Dave Kocak

Untiliwin Press
Buffalo,NY

Published by Untiliwin Press, 63 Courier Blvd, Buffalo NY 14217

ISBN 13: 978-0-615-20143-6

Dedication

This book is dedicated to the McDevitts: Jack, Alyce Ann, John, and Aynn. They took me into their family before they knew if they liked me and never had the heart to kick me out, even when they found out how annoying I can truly be.

Acknowledgements

I'd like to thank all the people who made this book possible. Special mention to Bev and Dick Kirby for their insight and encouragement. To Jeff Jones, Maureen Anderson, Sue Ballard, and all my other proofreaders and editors, I appreciate the care and time you volunteered.

Thanks to Mike Gelen for a fantastic cover and Chris Charles for all his efforts on the layout.

I'd like to thank all my models: Andrea Sperry, Ryan and Josh Zuccala, Caroline and Michael Fredericks, Bonnie Murphy, Jay and Nicole McKee, Sue Teetzel, Kelly Kazprzak, and Linda Sheridan.

I'd like to thank all my friends and students in East Liverpool, Ohio, Southtowns Tennis Center, Village Glen, and Miller Tennis Center in Buffalo for teaching me at least as much as I taught you.

Finally, I thank my wife, Joanne, and my son, Jackson, for making it all worthwhile.

Table of Contents

Author's Note

This book is intended for both men and women, but more women will read it, just as more women take tennis lessons than men. I don't necessarily endorse that; it's just the way it is. I teach many more women than men, and consequently this book will be more specifically geared to women than men. Don't worry guys, there's plenty here for you, too.

In order to simplify the instructional sections of the book, I assume that everyone is right-handed. I did not want to make the distinction between righties and lefties over and over again, so even though I myself am left-handed, I assume all of you are righties. Left-handed people are used to translating right-handed speech into left-handed speech anyway.

This book need not be read in the order in which it is laid out. The section labeled "Foundation" ends the part of the book best read as it is written, but even then, feel free to jump around at will. You don't have to read the entire book before you can read about what type of racquet to buy or how to play doubles.

Finally, I hope by the time you have finished reading, I have answered, at least in part, all or most of your questions about the entire tennis experience. More importantly, I hope you have learned a whole lot of new questions to ask, many of which can be answered only by you.

Introduction

It is surely a great calamity for a human being to have no obsessions.
Robert Bly

My wife expressed an interest in a "Journey" pendant for Valentine's Day. I never know what to get her, so off to the jewelry store I go. Advertised prices for this much-hyped item were "From $99 to $599." I've never purchased jewelry before except for an engagement ring 20 years ago, and that, I got through a friend. After looking at the pendants for several minutes, the only difference I could see between the $99 pendant and the $599 pendant was 500 bucks! Was the inexpensive one too cheap? Was the expensive one a rip off? I didn't know, nor could someone give me enough information and confidence to make an intelligent decision and buy what my wonderful, loving wife wanted for Valentine's Day. She got a box of chocolates and some flowers instead. And that's why I'm writing this tennis book!

You see, I don't know anything about jewelry, but I do know something about tennis. Heck, after thirty years, I know a lot about tennis. I may not know everything there is to know about tennis, I just know everything you need to know. I know that for every person who actually signs up for tennis lessons, or buys a racket and starts to play the game, there are ten who say "I always wanted to play tennis" or "I used to play a little as a kid and wanted to get back into it, but wasn't sure how to do it." I also know that far too many of those who do attempt the game quit without giving themselves a fair chance to become competent players. They get discouraged because the game is harder than they thought, and it really isn't much fun just chasing the #$%&$ balls all around the @##% court.

For all those people who are beginning or returning to the game or who are thinking about it, but not sure how to go about it or what to expect, this book is for you.

Tennis is a wonderful game and is truly a sport for a lifetime, but it is usually not an instant gratification game. It takes a little time to acquire the skills that will allow you to enjoy this great game to its fullest. If you don't think you are athletic enough, or don't know what to expect, you are likely to quit before you ever give yourself a chance to succeed. I don't want that to happen. By explaining what to expect, what you need to know, and how to get the necessary skills to succeed and enjoy the game, I strongly believe I can make you a tennis player for life.

At the least, I would very much like to try.

And I hope you have a few laughs along the way.

And there's no Math.

Chapter 1
You Were Born To Play This Game!

> Everyone is an athlete. The only difference is that some
> of us are in training, and some are not.
> **Dr. George Sheehan**

You have been preparing to play this game all your life. Whether it was playing catch with your Dad, or playing with dolls, or playing Little League baseball, or doing a six month stretch in Juvie, or raising a family, the skills you have acquired up to this point, properly applied, will help in your development as a tennis player. It's like those college credits they give you for life experience.

I guess this means you're not the rank beginner you thought you were. Hey, things are looking better already.

Unfortunately (or fortunately), some things are more valuable than others. Sports involving balls and sticks are helpful, those involving bouncing balls, even more so. The following chart will show you some of your life skills that will translate to tennis. I'm sure there are others.

Life Experience Chart

Alive and breathing	1 pt.	It's really all you need to start.
Played baseball or softball	5 pts.	Groundstrokes are like hitting, serving is like throwing, volley is like catching. You hit the trifecta.
Played basketball	3 pts.	Many of the movements are the same, plus ball sense and footwork.

Played chess	1 pt.	Strategy and thinking ahead are important.
Played with dolls	1 pt.	Social skills good for doubles
Spanked your kids	1 pt.	Spanking motion similar to a forehand.
Backhand slap your kids or spouse	1 pt.	Motion similar to backhand. Would be 2 pts., have to deduct for time spent in jail.
Started your own successful company	2 pts.	Have to pay for those lessons somehow.
Married a doctor or lawyer	2 pts.	See above.
Wash the car	2 pts.	Circular "wax on" motion similar to good forehand preparation (See "Karate Kid" movie for details).
Chop down trees	2 pts.	Chopping motion similar to slice groundstrokes and volleys.
Log splitter for the railroad	3 pts.	But you're not Abraham Lincoln, are you?
Can ride a bicycle	0 pts.	Editor's Note: Author never had a bike as a kid. He still has some issues to work out.
Balance your checkbook	1 pt.	Prepare you for the inevitable frustration at the pace of your progress. Don't worry, world class players have all felt the same frustration.
Peel potatoes	1 pt.	Peeling motion almost like a forehand or backhand slice.
A cookbook, a kitchen = a culinary masterpiece	1 pt.	The ability to follow directions good for any endeavor.
Can change a flat tire	1 pt.	Wrist strength to loosen lug nuts excellent for racquet control.
Playing catch with your kids or parents	2 pts.	Good for ball sense and hand-eye skills.
Get someone else to change your flat tire (no money or sex involved)	2 pts.	Negotiating skills good for any and all match or league controversies.
New York, or other major city pedestrian	1 pt.	Dodging in and out amongst all that traffic has to be good for footwork and quickness.

TOTAL:

0-1 pt – Alive, but barely

2-10 pts – You can play this game

11-30 pts – You have prepared well, my child

31-33 pts – Can't wait to read your book

Chapter 2
Physics or Why We Fail

Tennis seems innocently simple to those who are outside the fence looking in.
Vic Braden

Tennis is a simple game. Tennis is not an easy game, but it is a simple game. If it was complicated, a sixteen year old (Martina Hingis) could never have been the #1 player in the world. The physics of tennis are simple: get your racket behind and through the ball at the appropriate angle to send it over the net and to the desired spot on the court. It sounds marvelously easy, doesn't it? And those handsome men with their foreign names and sexy accents, and those pony-tailed girls in their cute outfits make it look just that easy, don't they?

Well, if that's what you think my friends, I'm afraid you've got Trouble, trouble, trouble (A clear rip-off of "The Music Man"). That's Trouble with a capital T and that rhymes with P and that stands for Physics! To hit that ball seems a simple thing. All that is required is that when that ball comes off your opponent's racquet you immediately assess:

    A) the direction of the ball
    B) the speed of the ball
    C) the spin of the ball and, therefore,
    D) where you need to be to hit that ball

Oh, and by the way, friend, while you were doing all that, did you remember to prepare your racket so that when you arrived at that magic spot you were ready to hit it? And I don't mean just hit it, friend, I mean hit it to a spot in that court where you'll win the point or at the very least where you won't give your opponent an easy opportunity to win it. And did I mention that if the racquet face is angled down 3 degrees too much the ball will go in the net or if it's angled up 3 degrees too much it will sail out?

Now, my friends, do you see why two million people take up tennis every year and 1.7 million of them quit before the fuzz is off their first can of balls?

But that's not you, friend, no, that's not you. (You bought this book!)

That fuzz on the ball is our saving grace and physics can work in our favor, for when those racquet strings meet that fuzz, they keep that ball on the racquet for 3 to 7 thousandths of a second. That may not seem like a lot, but it's enough time to control the ball and change its direction and maybe add some spin, and that spin means control, and that's Control with a capital C. According to Bernoulli's Principle (don't ask), if you can make the ball spin in the direction you hit it, the spin will force the ball downward, allowing you to hit the ball hard and high over the net and still come down into the court! How sweet is that? That's how the pros do it, friends. And that's how we'll do it. Physics may be our friend after all.

Newton and Einstein taketh away and Bernoulli (don't ask) giveth back!

Chapter 3
Neurology, or Why we Succeed

Skill to do comes of doing.
Ralph Waldo Emerson

It blows me away at how well this game is played. With all the actions and decisions to be made in mere tenths of a second, I can barely imagine how the pros play the game, and yet they do. Heck, I play a pretty good game myself, and I know I'm nothing special. You can too, and here's why:

Every skill exists as a neurological circuit that has to be formed and optimized. Every lining up of the ball, every swing of the racket helps form that circuit. Over and over again neurons fire with each movement and a substance called myelin wraps around each nerve fiber, insulating and controlling the impulses along those nerve wires. Complex skills take a long time to master as the myelin slowly wraps around the nerve fibers, up to 40 or 50 times in a process that can take days or weeks.

This is how these skills are formed. How are they optimized? Technique, technique, technique. The brain does not intuitively know how to play tennis. Any walk through the public courts makes this obvious as you observe the many and varied ways people think to hit a tennis ball. Unfortunately, many of those players do it their way over and over again, wrapping that myelin thicker and thicker around those nerve fibers (Practice makes permanent); one day they awake and realize they are not improving because the physics (oh, that again) of their bad technique makes improvement too slow or near impossible. Then they come to me and say "Fix this," hoping to undo months or years of incorrect technique in an hour.

17

You have not taken that path (You bought this book!). Repetition of proper technique builds the foundation of a solid tennis game. Progress is not measured in days or months but in thousands of correctly struck balls.

But don't worry, as I said earlier, "You were born to play this game!"

Common Tennis Terms You Need to Know

Baseline – Endline of the court. This is not called the "Service Line"

Rally – A series of shots back and forth across the net. Not to be confused with "Volley" - any ball struck before it bounces. You can have a "Volley" rally, a series of volleys back and forth.

Let – Any serve that hits the net and goes into the service box. This results in a replay of the serve. Also, any disruption of play in the middle of the point, usually for safety reasons, such as a ball rolling onto your court. The server always gets two serves after a disruption of play. *A "Let" is **never** played because a player could not tell if a shot was in or out. The point always goes to the other player when a player cannot be certain about a line call.*

Open Face – Top of racquet tilted backward, racquet face is "open" to the sky. Shot is more likely to sail high or be sliced.

Closed Face – Top of racquet tilted forward, face is directed downward. Shot is more likely to stay low and possibly hit with topspin.

Hitting Zone – From the knee to the waist. This is the ideal location for the ball when hitting groundstrokes (forehands or backhands).

Chapter 4
The Learning Curve

I don't care how good you play: you can find somebody who can beat you, and I don't care how bad you play: you can find somebody you can beat.
Harvey Penick

The talent, skills and experience you bring to tennis will determine your own learning curve; however, all tennis learning curves are similar. There are basically three phases to the curve. The initial phase establishes your starting point and the angle of your initial improvement. The more skill, talent, and experience you bring, the sharper the angle and the longer this line will be.

If you have played other sports and are athletically experienced, this will be the time of your greatest improvement. Thoughts like "How long has this game been going on?" and "If only I had started younger, I could be a pro now!" will be dancing through your head.

If you don't bring much to the table in terms of skill, talent, and experience, this will be the time of your greatest disappointment. Thoughts like "They make it look so easy on TV." and "I can't believe I'm this bad!" will be dancing (exploding?) in your head.

Not to worry. This initial phase, which lasts a couple of months or a few thousand balls, only sets the baseline, a starting point, for your development as a tennis player. **Reality check:** Phase two is where the work begins. However sharp or dull the curve has been, scale that down a little bit and this is the path we will be on for another couple of months or a couple thousand balls.

Phase three is the rest of your tennis life. It is a slow upward progression, occasionally jumping upward as some skill is mastered or dipping downward for any one of many reasons (injury, changing a stroke, playing less, falling in love, going to jail). The very good news is that **skills once acquired cannot be taken away.** Let me repeat this. *Skills once acquired cannot be taken away.* Once you understand the bounce and spin of the ball, a forehand stroke, the geometry of the court, it never goes away.

Skills once learned are yours for life, so don't worry so much about the pace of your progress. Each little bit of skill sits atop all those other little bits of skill and eventually you're sitting on top of a mountain. Each day, you are a little bit better than the day before, not so much that you would notice, but over time, each little bit adds up. Occasionally you run into someone who hasn't played with you in six months or a year, and they can see the improvement in your game. Sometimes they even compliment you on it. I see it all the time.

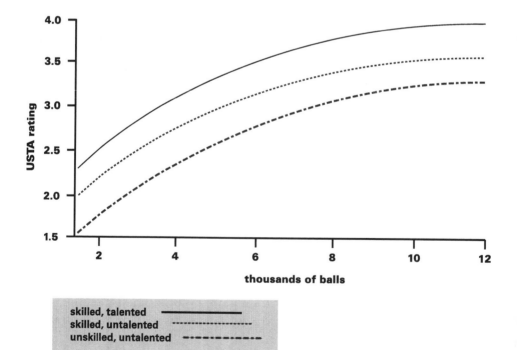

A friend and regular opponent, Mike, who was a bit better than me before I went away to teach for a year, was my opponent in the semifinals of a local tournament. I played reasonably well and won 6-2, 6-2 but was disappointed because I felt Mike had not played very well, and I wanted to know if I had improved to the point where I was better than him. We shook hands, and in a nice way I remarked that it was too bad that he hadn't played his usual game and that we hadn't had a better match. I was shocked to hear him say that he thought he had played pretty well but that I had gotten that much better. An easy finals win against another previously difficult opponent confirmed his analysis. So you see, even I was fooled by the slow, miniscule, relentless improvement in my game.

Common Tennis Terms You Need to Know

No Man's Land – The area of the court from the service line to the baseline, so named because no man (or woman) should be standing there. Psst – *That's where all the balls bounce. If you are in there, they are all bouncing at your feet.*

Cross court – Diagonally from where you are. A cross court rally would be forehand to forehand, or backhand to backhand with the ball traveling over the middle of the net.

Down-the-Line – A shot perpendicular to the net and parallel with the sideline. Typically the pro says "Hit down-the-line" and the student asks "Down which line? There's so many." A down-the-line forehand would go to your opponent's backhand.

Inside Out – Neither cross court or down-the-line, an inside out shot travels in the opposite direction of the cross court, for example, a forehand from the middle of the court to your opponent's backhand corner.

Deuce Court – The right hand court, so named because the "Deuce" point is always played in that court.

Ad Court – The left hand court, so named because the "Aaaah, you can figure it out!"

Chapter 5

Tennis Competence

> Genius is reducing the
> complicated to the simple.
> **C. W. Ceran**

Tennis competence requires two things: **ball sense and racquet skills.** Yes, to be very good requires a few other things like good footwork and court coverage, decent strategy, power, a killer shot, and a competitive spirit, but if you were looking for all those things, you wouldn't have bought *this* book. **Ball sense and racquet skills.** That's it. And you may already have them and not be aware of them. Maybe you played softball or catch with your kid or come from a country where they still beat rugs on a clothesline with something that resembles a tennis racquet from the 1930s. The earlier chart may have already alerted you to some hidden skills you have acquired to help you in these tasks.

Ball sense. The ability to quickly judge the destination of a struck ball and position yourself to maximize the possibility of hitting it back. The one word that makes this problematical is the word "quickly." Notice that I did not write "quickly run" or "quickly move" to the ball, although that ability is nice to have. The correct phrase is **"quickly judge"** where to move, for if you are positioned properly (and you will be after chapter 25), getting to the ball is not the problem you may imagine it to be.

How fast is it coming? How deep is it hit? How high will it be when it gets to me? are the three questions that must be answered, and answered quickly. Pros do this extremely well, beginners, not so well. Just watch a class of young beginners as they are fed balls from the opposite side of the court. Watch how they run up for the

23

high balls, only to jump helplessly as the balls bounce over their heads. Answering one of those three questions incorrectly usually results in a missed shot, for pros as well as beginners. Roger Federer made 33 unforced forehand errors against Rafael Nadal in the 2007 French Open final largely because he misjudged the height and speed of Nadal's heavily top-spinned shots. Maybe someday that can be your excuse!

How does one acquire ball sense? Seeing lots and lots and lots of balls: balls with spin, flat shots, mishit shots. If you have already done this, you are one step ahead of the game. If you have not, then let's get at it!

Racquet skills. Your ability to control the racquet and strike the ball with the correctly angled racquet face will largely determine your success as a tennis player. This can be proven by walking into the lobby of any tennis club in the world and picking out the best players, or the worst, before they walk on court and start hitting. It can't be done. Once they start hitting, all is revealed. Young, old, short, tall, thin, fat – it's all about the racquet and how it's used.

How does one acquire these "racquet skills?" Hitting lots and lots and lots of balls? Nope. Hitting lots and lots and lots of balls....here it comes, wait for it.....**PROPERLY!** Kinda like "Practice doesn't make perfect; perfect practice makes perfect!"

Racquet skills and ball skills improve together. Every time a ball crosses the net, it is another opportunity to practice both skills. See, you just improved twice as fast.

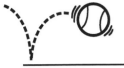

Chapter 6
Equipment

> I'll let my racquet do the talking.
> **John McEnroe**

I'm not a big equipment guy. Rather than spending your money on the newest racquet or frequent restrings, I think your money is better spent on lessons or court time. It is ironic that today's equipment makes the game so much easier to play than in the 70s or before and yet more people aren't playing. With that in mind, here are a few thoughts on the subject.

Racquets: Until the 1970s all tennis racquets were made of wood, were very similar in their size and weight and there were only two types of string, gut, which played great but couldn't get wet and cost a fortune, and basic nylon. All that changed in the 1970's. Wooden racquets would fatigue and break, so most players replaced their racquets every few years. With the advent of new materials; graphite, ceramics, titanium, Kevlar, racquets stopped breaking. Heck, they even stopped getting tired and spongy. A player who didn't hit the ball too hard could keep a racquet forever. The manufacturers panicked, but also saw a great opportunity. The new racquets were made in molds rather than many wooden pieces glued together. The first racquet out of the mold cost a fortune, but every one after that was pretty inexpensive. The only way to get a player to give up his old racquet and part with some of his lesson money was to make a better racquet. That they have done. Since the 1970's, racquets have been getting bigger, lighter, more powerful, and more forgiving on off-center hits. Every few years there is a technology bump or jump, and to stay competitive you cannot be too many generations behind.

Strings. I don't think I know an amateur player who plays with gut strings today. The synthetic strings have evolved just as the racquets have, although their effect has not been so dramatic. Different strings emphasize different things: playability, string life, power, stress on the arm. Different tensions can also enhance power, control, or relieve stress on the elbow.

Shoes. Everyone knows that Air Jordans can cost $200 and that your grandparents owned maybe one pair of "sneakers" that they used for any and all sports activities. We live in an age of consumer selection. What to do? What to do?

If you are just starting tennis and you do not have TENNIS shoes, cross trainers will do for awhile. No need to break the bank all at once. Running shoes are never acceptable. They are far too likely to cause or not prevent an ankle injury. Running shoes are never acceptable, and just put out of your mind playing in socks or barefoot. I probably didn't need to say that last part, huh?

This I do need to say. In horseracing they have a saying, "No foot, no horse!" Get a good pair of tennis shoes. And stop wearing those high heels! That goes for you ladies, too.

Let's start with racquets. As I've said, racquets just keep getting better and better. An inexpensive racquet from a tennis shop (K-Mart, Wal-Mart and Dick's are not tennis shops) is better than the best racquet from 20 years ago. A racquet in the $75 - $125 range is a good place to start, even better if it's that $200 racquet that was so hot a couple years ago but is now being closed out to make way for the new line. (You ladies of fashion know how that works.)

> **WARNING:** The racquet with the biggest head may not be ideal for the beginner who mis-hits a lot. The lightest or most powerful model is not necessarily right for the physically weak player who thinks this will compensate for their frailties. The racquet with the big head may be very hard to maneuver, while the power model may give you too much power and not enough control, intimidating you from using a complete stroke. There are exceptions, of course, but you are probably not one of them.

Grip size is important. Racquet grips range from 4" to 4 5/8", with most players either 4 1/4, 4 3/8, or 4 1/2. When you wrap your hand around the grip there should be a one finger (I don't know which one) gap between your fingers and your hand. If in doubt, remember that it is always easier to make a grip bigger than it is to make it smaller.

Most players keep that starter racquet until they seem to hit a plateau in their development. A new racquet seems like a likely jumpstart to rejuvenate their own personal Wimbledon Express. If this is where you are, I strongly suggest you try several demo racquets from your local pro shop. Try several manufacturers first to get a feel for which line of racquets you might like. Narrow it down within that line after that, always keeping in mind that the $300 racquet will probably feel better than the $150 model. A better grade of string might be worth trying also.

If your racquet comes factory strung, have someone check the strings to see if they are tight enough. If your racquet is unstrung, a lower grade synthetic strung in the middle of the recommended tension range should be fine. If you already have arm problems, using a softer string, or stringing it slightly looser, or both, may help. Ask the stringer for advice.

Restringing. One day you are going to break a string. Until that day comes, you will often ask the question (usually after a bad day) "Does this need restrung?" Strings that are too loose do a very poor job of controlling the ball and therefore need replaced. If they are not too loose, I recommend you keep them until they break, or one year, whichever comes first. You know how the oil change guys tell you to change your engine oil every 3,000 miles, but the manufacturer says every 5,000 to 7,000 miles? Same idea for racquet stringers.

Tennis Balls. Most tennis balls sold in the U.S. are either Wilson or Penn with brands like Dunlop and Gamma getting a smaller share of the market. All these companies make balls for specific court surfaces; clay, synthetic or hard courts. I doubt that you would notice much difference between any of them unless you are a pretty good player. Tennis balls come in plastic cans that are pressurized. You should hear a whoosh of escaping air as you open them. **Balls you**

are interested in buying do not come in net bags or boxes. Pressurized balls have a higher, more consistent bounce than balls in the Super Saver net bags. Ball sense requires that the bounce of the ball be consistent, otherwise how do you predict what is coming at you? Alas, nothing lasts forever and even the pressurized balls lose their life. If you are unsure whether a ball is dead or not, place it in your hand and try to push your fingers into the center. If you can push in an inch or more, retire it to your ball hopper and use it for serving practice. There are quality pressureless balls, but they tend to feel heavy on the racquet and most teaching pros think they are an invitation to tennis elbow. Tennis balls are the low tech economic miracle of my lifetime. In 1972 when I began playing tennis, balls cost $2 a can. Today you can still find first rate balls for the same price. What else can you say that about?

> USTA league and tournament matches always use a new can of balls, often using a new can if a match goes to a third set. Pro matches change balls after the first seven games and every nine games thereafter. Even within a match, balls tend to slow down, thus the need for frequent changes at the Pro level.

> Tennis balls hit into the stands during a pro match are not "souvenirs" and should be returned to the court when asked. Don't be the guy on TV pushing away some youngster to get an errant ball and then running one step ahead of security out of the stadium. It's just not worth it!

Racquets for children: See the section on Tennis for Kids.

Chapter 7

The Foundation

> I make mistakes sometimes, but on the whole I am becoming an expert.
> **Marat Safin**

Just like the three little pigs, or is it the seven dwarfs, your tennis foundation determines the potential of your game. Build your game on bricks and not on straw. Attention to the basics now makes for a smooth learning curve and very little backtracking later. These are the essentials.

Continental

Eastern Forehand

The Grips. You may have noticed that the grip on a tennis racquet is not round. If it was round, you'd never be sure where the racquet face was without looking. Since that would never do, the racquet has four sides, and four angled bevels adjacent to each side. If you put the racquet on edge and position your hand so that the V formed by your thumb and forefinger is placed on the left side bevel, you have the **Continental Grip.** This is also the grip most people would use to hammer a nail. (If you hammer with a different grip, please don't ask me to hold the nail.) Turn the racquet a quarter turn to the left and you now have an **Eastern Forehand Grip.** Move it again so that the "V" is now near the bottom right bevel and you have a **Western Grip.**

29

Between the Eastern and the Western is a Semi-Western Grip. The three main grips are Western, Eastern, and Continental. The Western or the Semi-Western is a forehand grip. Most big forehands today are Semi-Western or Western.

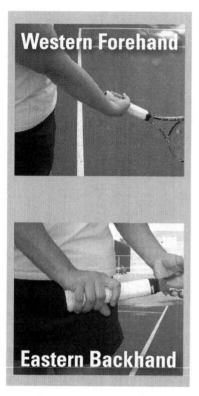

The Eastern Forehand Grip is still quite acceptable as it more easily presents the best racquet face to hit the ball. A quarter counter clockwise turn is the **Eastern Backhand** which once again presents a flat racket face for the backhand. One handed or two handed, most backhand grips will not be far away from an Eastern Grip.

The Continental Grip is preferred for serves, overheads, volleys, and sliced groundstrokes. It is not particularly good for topspin groundstrokes and not very good at all for high balls, but it is ideal for serves and overheads because it allows for maximum wrist action. The Continental grip is also ideal for volleys, because no grip change is needed from forehand to backhand.

The correct grip for the correct stroke allows the stroke to develop properly and without limitations. There is nothing harder to change than your grip. Phrases like *"Ooh, this doesn't feel natural"* or *"I don't think I like this!"* or *"See you later, Buddy!"* often follow the least little grip change. Allowances can be made in the beginning based on strength or age (weak wrist) but always with an eye towards moving to the proper grip.

If you didn't follow the written description of each grip (I know I didn't, and I wrote it), just try to duplicate the hand positions in the pictures.

The Ready Position. The ready position is simply that position which gives you the best chance to move to and hit the ball. You should be on the balls of your feet, your feet shoulder width apart with your racket above your wrist and in front of you. Your grip is whatever is comfortable and loose. Do not squeeze the racket. Your left hand is the key. If you have a one-handed backhand, your left hand will be on the throat of the racket, three fingertips on one side of the throat, thumb on the other side, index fingertip against the strings. With a two-handed backhand, the left hand will be just above the right hand.

One-Handed

Two-Handed

Use of the Left Hand. The left hand performs three important functions: First, it supports the racket in between shots allowing your right hand to rest. Secondly, your left, and not your right hand, makes all grip changes. The left hand moves the racket inside a loose right hand, smoothly making all grip changes. This is much easier than trying to make them with the right. Try it. Thirdly, the left hand lines up the ball and balances you on the forehand groundstroke. Most of us have two arms, two legs, two eyes, two ears, all divided right down the middle. Okay, not you, Cyclops, but most of us. When one arm does something, the other usually does something to offset that motion and keep us in balance. As the right arm goes back for a forehand, the left needs to move forward at the same time. As the right arm swings, the left moves to balance that swing. Good forehands need good balancing action by the left hand. In order to get back into the ready position, the racquet must return to the left hand.

The Wrist. You may have heard that tennis is not a wristy game. Tennis is a very wristy game. Unlike squash and racquetball, the wrist is not used to generate racquet head speed and thus power; the tennis wrist is used to control the racket. That is a problem for many of you, because your wrist is not used to being used at all. Test: Point your right arm downward, racquet in hand also pointing vertically to the ground. Now pick up the racket with your wrist so that the racquet head is parallel with the ground. Most women and almost all children will pick up the racquet with their forearm (first picture) and now the forearm is parallel with the ground, avoiding using the wrist to control the racquet. We naturally compensate for our weaknesses. Many experienced players have no tennis wrist because they have worked around using it from Day One and have never strengthened it. We will focus on using the wrist to control the racquet. That which we use grows stronger, that which we avoid stays the same or weakens.

Incorrect: Forearm holds the racquet   Correct: Wrist holds the racquet

The Hitting Zone. The ideal place to hit a groundstroke is between the knee and the waist, the natural drop of your arms. This is the Hitting Zone. Our ball sense should be trying to figure out a way to get the ball into or close to our hitting zone. Most matches are won by the player who gets the most balls in this zone. Think about it. If the balls are all too high, too low, too wide, or too close, how successful can you be? Of course, your opponent might have something to do with this problem.

The Contact Point. Good serves, groundstrokes, volleys, and over-heads are all hit in front of the body. I can't emphasize this enough. Contact the ball in front. Whether you hit open stance (feet almost equidistant from the net) or step into the shot, your contact point should be in front. Good serves are hit with your body weight going forward, and that is very hard to do with the ball behind you. The same is true for volleys and overheads. A myriad of bad habits (and arm problems) come from contacting the ball late.

Early Preparation. Early preparation does not necessarily mean taking the racquet back early. It does mean lining up the ball and starting your racquet preparation. You don't really run with your racquet all the way back. You run balanced, which usually implies the racquet partially back to the side you are moving but not fully extended. Most groundstrokes by most players are hit in rhythm: a step, a shoulder turn, and then the complete stroke.

Adjustments. Tennis is a game of adjustments, not of absolutes. Always and Never are rarely in the tennis vocabulary. The answer to most technical questions is "It depends." How far should I take my racquet back? It depends! Should I step into the ball or hit with an open stance? It depends! Should I hit cross court or down the line? It depends. Does this tennis dress make me look fat? Does this dress make me look fat? Hellooo....is anybody there? (Some questions just shouldn't be answered.)

Common Tennis Terms you Need to Know

M or W?, P or D?, Up or Down? – The spin of the racquet at the beginning of the match decides who serves and on which side. These are simply the designations on the bottom of most racquets, **W** for Wilson, upside down it is an **M**. **P** for Prince, upside down it is a **d**. For all others, it is whatever insignia is on the bottom of the racquet. I suppose you could flip a coin, but then you wouldn't have the excuse "I left my wallet in the locker room," when it was time to pay for post-match drinks. You have three choices should you win the spin: 1) Serve or receive 2) start on a particular side 3) let the other team choose. You cannot choose serve and side as in *"We'll serve first from uphill with the wind at our backs!"*

Bye – When there are extra players for a league, those that are not scheduled to play are said to have a "Bye." When there are an uneven number of players in a tournament, one or more players automatically move into the second round. They are said to receive a "bye" and that is what is written on the line for their opponent on the official draw sheet. One new player looking at the draw sheet saw "Bye" listed six or seven times and noted "That Bye family has an awful lot of tennis players."

Chapter 8
Taking the Terror out of Topspin

Be bold. If you are going to make an error, make
a doozy. And don't be afraid to hit the ball.
Billie Jean King

I don't believe that spin, and especially topspin, is only found in XY
Male Chromosomes, although it is true that adult women seem to
take a little longer to figure out spin and how to hit it. I attribute that
to a background that didn't include Little League baseball or something similar. In the 50's we all understood backspin by throwing
hula hoops and having them spin back to us. The deprived youth
of later generations will somehow have to compensate for that de-
ficiency. Spin is a learned concept and some of us haven't learned it
yet, until today.

Think of a tennis ball as one of those atomic models made out of tin-
ker toys with the nucleus in the center and the electrons on the outside attached to the nucleus by rods. (You said no math, but science
is even worse.) To hit the ball flat, you should try to hit the nucleus.
To hit with spin, you are only interested in the electrons. Most of you
didn't even realize a tennis ball had electrons.

Topspin. A ball that rotates in the direction it is struck has topspin.
The top of the ball is moving faster than the bottom of the ball, and
Bernoulli (remember him?) says that makes the pressure on the top
greater than the pressure on the bottom, and therefore it is forced
downward. The arc of the ball does not look like a rainbow, as a flat
shot does. It more closely resembles a rainbow that runs out of energy, like when you give your kids a project.

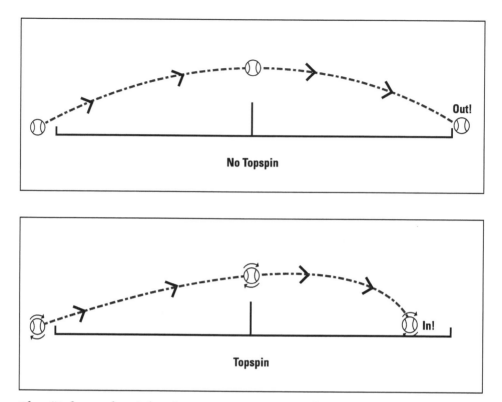

The flight path of the first rainbow sends the ball beyond the baseline while the second ball lands inside the baseline, and that, boys and girls, is how the pros keep the ball in play indefinitely.

To hit topspin you must do two things. First, you must swing low to high, from below the contact point to above the contact point. It follows then, that to hit topspin, I must drop my racquet below the contact point. It should be done in a way that a casual observer can see your racquet dropping below the ball, not suddenly swooping down from above your head and magically getting under the ball. You shouldn't change your stroke, just drop the racquet lower to accommodate a more "low to high" swing. Secondly, you must keep your wrist firm in the horizontal plane. Your racquet face cannot brush the ball if the wrist is driving it forward. In other words, your palm should stay parallel with the net. If you do just these two things, your shots will have topspin. Great Topspin? Not yet.

Most shots have a combination of drive and spin. A shot that is all drive will be inconsistent. A shot that is all spin will lack pace and depth and be fairly easy to handle. As I said, doing just the two things above gives you topspin. To get more topspin you need to work the electrons, not the nucleus, and you need to generate a little more racquet head speed. Since you have a joint in the middle of your arm (your elbow), your lower arm can do some things on its own as it goes along for the ride with your upper arm. Your forearm can swing the racquet in a vertical motion, brushing the back of the ball, as your shoulder and upper arm are swinging through the ball. Your forearm concentrates on the electrons as your upper arm swings through the nucleus. The faster the racquet head brush, the more intense the spin. The faster the arm through the ball, the faster the shot. Two separate motions working in harmony to produce a fast shot with lots of spin.

Different shots require different amounts of speed and spin. For example, a sharp crosscourt angle requires lots of spin to force the ball down onto the court before it goes wide. An attempted winner down the line needs pace more than spin to get past your opponent. All is possible with practice.

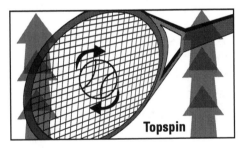

Underspin, Backspin, Slice. Good news: all three terms are used to describe the same thing. With backspin, the ball is rotating in the opposite direction from topspin, and therefore the pressure on the bottom is greater than the pressure on the top, making the ball rise rather than drop.

Backspin is more complicated than topspin, which requires you hit the ball with a flat racquet face – one angle. Backspin can be hit with anything from a slightly open to an extremely open racquet face, depending on what you are trying to accomplish. Once again, we are trying to work the electrons more than the nucleus. The swing is slightly high to low with a somewhat open racquet face. *How open? It depends!* Chapters ahead on slice backhand, approach shot and dropshot will give you a clearer image of slice. Once again, play around. Experiment. You'll figure it out.

Balls that spin bounce differently from balls that do not. Topspin makes the ball bounce higher and jump forward more than a flat shot. Underspin shots slide lower than normal and when hit vertically, do not want to go forward at all. With enough underspin, they will bounce backwards, kinda like that hula hoop. You already know this from the time when a soft high shot was hit with underspin and you didn't know it; and you were waiting for it to bounce to you, and it didn't, and you then lunged forward looking stupid and didn't hit the ball. Remember that time like it was yesterday? Ooohhh, it was yesterday. Never mind.

Remember, tennis is, first and foremost, two things: ball sense and racquet skills. You need to recognize the type of spin the ball has in order to properly line yourself up for the shot. If you don't know where the ball is going to be, how can you make a good shot?

Topspin – the racquet swings low to high with a flat face, the ball bounces up and forward.

Slice – racquet face is open, swing is somewhat high to low, ball slides lower. If hit vertically, the ball does not want to go forward.

Chapter 9
The Forehand

Forehands are as simple as "Wax on, wax off" for you Karate Kid" fans or rotating your palm parallel with the side fence. The grip is eastern or semi-western.

Step one. From the ready position, turn your palm out (figure 1). Your racquet should be vertical with the strings facing the net. This angle of the wrist to your arm should be maintained throughout the shot (figure 2).

Step two. Shoulder turn with racquet still vertical and strings facing side wall. Left hand out in front to line up the ball and balance you (figure 2).

figure 1

figure 2

Step three. Racquet back as far as you wish or as far as you have time to take it and still hit the ball in front.

Step four. Drop your racquet and your hand (if possible) below the contact point and then up and through the ball (about where your left hand is) and then into your left hand and somewhere by or over your left shoulder. This is all in one smooth motion. If the ball is slow and easy or you have prepared quickly, save steps three and four so they can be executed without any stops. (figures 3, 4, and 5).

| figure 3 | figure 4 | figure 5 |

If you think of the arm motion as a circular waxing motion with your palm facing the side, you've got it.

How high or low do I take the racquet? How far back do I take it? It depends! How high is my contact point? How much time do I have?

Tara's Student Notebook

He's Tough. He wants me to make the perfect loop. Not a good loop, a perfect loop. He says "Form follows function! If you want to be consistent, you have to have a consistent, low-to-high stroke with a firm wrist." When I did it right, I could feel it. And when I did it right, the ball went in. I just didn't do it right that often.

Footwork. Your last step will either be a right foot step to the side-line (open stance) or a step with your left foot toward the net (square stance) but not a left foot across toward the sideline (closed stance). Anyway, contact should be in front, but you already knew that.

| open stance | square stance | closed or crossover (bad) |

Common Tennis Terms You Need to Know

Drill Clinic – A Pro supervised hitting session usually open to all players of a certain skill level where, through a series of drills, you can work on your strokes, movement and match play.

Round Robin – 1. A fat bird. 2. A playing format that features switching opponents, partners, or both, usually at a social event.

Tennis Obsession – To play tennis more than loved ones think is appropriate.

Self-Centered – See above.

Chapter 10

The Backhand

> The consequences of an act affect the probability of it happening again.
> **B. F. Skinner**

Backhands are either hit one-handed or two-handed. Two-handed backhands are almost always hit flat or with topspin. One-handed backhands are either hit flat, with topspin, or they are sliced. The slice backhand is a distinctly different shot from the topspin backhand.

Two-handed Backhand. Most beginners, adults and children, start with a two handed backhand. Most beginners have no backhand muscles and a weak wrist and the two-hander is much easier. Often inexperienced players find their two-handed backhands stronger and more consistent than their forehands. With experience, many players switch from a two-hander to the one-hander but rarely does the reverse happen.

The grip varies with the right hand being anywhere from an Eastern forehand to an Eastern backhand grip. The left hand is also adjustable. The backswing can be looped (figure 1) or straight back, but the important thing is that the racquet face be slightly closed or flat on the backswing (figure 2.) Experiment with the grips a bit to make this comfortable. Observe the results. Are the balls flying high or are they consistently in the net? If necessary, adjust the grip or the swing until you get a nice low-to-high shot.

figure 1   figure 2   figure 3   figure 4

The contact point is in front of the body but not excessively so (figure 3). It has to be comfortable for the left as well as the right arm. Ideally, the ball is in "the hitting zone." If the ball is lower, bend your knees and/or drop your racquet head below your wrist. If the ball is higher, adjust your backswing upwards so you can still hit through the ball.

Think of the two hands having different jobs. The right hand is the power and the left is the controller. Try not to dominate the racquet with the left hand when you swing through the ball. Let it "go along for the ride," while still controlling the racquet face. Both hands should be over your right shoulder on the finish (figure 4).

That's it. It is simplicity itself. When you attempt to hit topspin, the left hand and arm will do most of the work, but the basic two-hander is very easy. It's amazing that it took Chris Evert and Jimmy Connors to make it popular; now the majority of players use it.

There are some advantages to a **one-handed backhand.** Those of you who are long and lean may swing freely with both arms, while those of us who are short and stocky (or just stocky) may not be comfortable hanging onto the racquet with both hands all the way through the shot. Your reach is also a little compromised with two hands. Deciding to use one hand or two takes a lot of factors into play, and there aren't any absolutes. Venus and Serena Williams, although sisters, have two very different body types and both are two-handed. Little Justine Henin has the best one-handed backhand in the game. Go figure! Let your Pro help you decide which is best for you.

figure 5

The one-handed backhand requires a little more wrist and forearm strength than any other shot. The grip is usually an **Eastern Backhand** (figure 5) or possibly a little more extreme. The ready position (figure 6) has the left hand on the throat of the racquet. The backswing is either a loop with the racquet about head high (similar to a forehand loop) or it is straight back at about mid-thigh (figure 7), which is the natural drop of the arms. Most players prefer some kind of loop backswing, better rhythm and more power. The left hand stays on the throat of the racquet until the racquet comes forward.

The contact point should be further in front than with the two-hander (figure 8). It is very hard to be late and effective, which makes the later contact point of the two-hander an important point in its favor. The racquet head rarely drops below the wrist and the finish is always above the wrist (figure 9). You can't drag the racquet through the shot.

figure 6   figure 7

figure 8   figure 9

The slice backhand is almost always hit one-handed. Two-handers may begin the shot with both hands on the racquet but may hit and finish with one. The grip is Continental, providing a slightly open racquet face (figure 10). The arm and body form a rectangle (figure 10) (body, upper arm, lower arm and laid-back wrist with racquet forming the four sides) with the front shoulder pointing at the net. The upper arm, lower arm, wrist, and racquet come towards the net in succession as the racquet face moves through the ball. The arms go from bent to straight (figure 11).

| figure 10 | figure 11 | figure 12 |

The racquet face is open. *How open? It depends:* Slightly open for higher balls, very open for low balls. The angle of the racquet face and the angle of attack must be coordinated to produce a shot at the right angle with the right amount of pace and spin. *What?* Two things are in play: the angle of the racquet face and the angle of the swing. It's not as simple as topspin, where the racquet face is just flat. It is one of those shots that require you to play around with it, *A LOT!*

Players with a good topspin backhand still slice their backhands in certain situations: on very low balls, very high balls, running forward for a shot, and for those shots they are likely to be hitting late. Slice backhands take a little less effort than topspin and are very effective in countering topspin, as you do not have to change the rotation of the ball.

Think about that one!

Try not to fool around with the racquet face through the contact area. You do not have perfect timing (nor do I) and cannot play with the ball on your strings like you are concertmaster at the New York Philharmonic. Remember, .003 to .007 seconds is all you get. **Ball sense and racquet skills** will help you make the correct early decision relating to angle of the face and angle of the swing. If you choose badly, your shot will be too *fluffy* or be driven into the bottom of the net. *Learn from your errors. Make adjustments.*

Try not to finish with your racquet pointing to the side fence. You want to hit *through* the ball, not across it (figure 12). The more your racquet and front shoulder finish towards the target, the longer you will be swinging through the ball.

The wrist and forearm strength required to hit good slice backhands will be easier if you also hit one-handed topspin backhands. That only makes sense. Two-handers struggle with the grip change and the wrist and forearm skills needed to keep the racquet face properly angled and controlled. As two-handers, those arm and wrist strengths, or lack of, were compensated for by the second hand. It's harder for two-handers, but possible and necessary.

John's Student Notebook

I had a good topspin two-handed backhand. I wanted to learn a slice for low balls, high balls, and approach shots. The good news: I learned it surprisingly quickly. The bad news: I move to the ball on the backhand side, and now I don't know which one to use. Reminds me of the ancient proverb (ancient?) "The man with two watches never knows what time it is."

Common Tennis Terms You Need to Know

Non-verbal line calls. Often the courts are too noisy to easily hear another person's line call. The three common non-verbal line calls are:

1. Hand slightly extended sidewards, palm facing down – Shot is **Good!**

2. Index finger pointing upwards – Shot is **Out!**

3. Middle finger pointing upwards. Shot is **Good!** but I'm calling it **Out!** because you cheated me on the last close call.

Tennis Fun Fact

One of the wonderful things about tennis is that you meet a marvelously wide cross section of very interesting people. I have played with generals, admirals, sports franchise owners, "celebrities," and in the 1970s occasionally played doubles with the mortician who prepared the body of the infamous gangster "Pretty Boy Floyd" after he was shot to death by eight FBI agents in East Liverpool, Ohio in 1938. Of course, that story has a lot of holes in it.

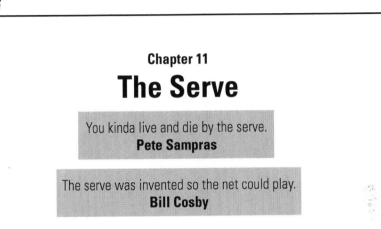

Chapter 11
The Serve

> You kinda live and die by the serve.
> **Pete Sampras**

> The serve was invented so the net could play.
> **Bill Cosby**

"OK. Now let me get this straight. You want me to throw the ball with my left hand while I simultaneously lift the racquet with my right hand and hit the ball I just threw. Now you want me to hit it where? In that diagonal box with the net in front of it? Now how am I supposed to do that?"

How, indeed? The serve is the most complex stroke. Fortunately, the serve is the only stroke that is not time constrained. You have all day (or at least a few seconds) to think about what you want to do, to get yourself lined up, and then to execute. It's the lining up that's going to make this easy or at least easier.

First I'd like you to hold the racquet up slightly in front of you and as high as you can reach. Take a ball with your left hand and toss it slightly higher than the racquet. This is how high you want to toss the ball. It's easier to reach that spot if the toss arm drops all the way down to the top of your left thigh.

The grip is **Continental.** If that is uncomfortable or if the first fifteen balls slice to the left, we will move closer to a forehand grip. Our eventual goal is to be Continental!

figure 1

Now let's line up. Figure 1 shows the correct basic starting position for the serve. Right foot is parallel with the baseline. Left foot is at a 45 degree angle to the baseline. **You should be able to draw a line through your toes into the middle of the service box.** Your shoulders and your racquet should also be along that line.

This is important: Hold the left palm open along the line of your left thigh and tuck your elbow in a little bit (should be noticeably awkward) right along the line of your left leg. This is to help you toss the ball along this line and not all over the court!

The bottom two fingers (pinky and ring fingers) of your left hand support the racquet so that it can be held loosely in the right hand. The serve is a wristy shot, and we don't want the arm all locked up.

figure 2

figure 3

That's an awful lot of things to think about. Let's try again.

A line through your toes toward the service box. Point your racquet to the court. Open your left palm and support the racquet with your bottom two fingers, nice and loose with the right hand.

Everyone can do that, no time pressure, just following directions. Next, (figure 2) as your toss arm drops to the top of your left thigh, your racquet arm drops down and past your body along that same line you've established toward the service box. As your toss arm tosses the ball (extend your arm as you release), your racket arm moves up and points your racket straight up to the sky so that both arms are extended upward (don't go crazy; your elbows are only shoulder high). This is your power position – your checkpoint (figure 3). From this position you have time to make a loop and accelerate the racket. You also have time to assess the situation. If the toss is bad or your timing and balance are off, this is the time to catch the ball and start over. If not, we drop and loop the racket and swing up and through the ball (figure 4 and 5).

The follow-through is to the left side of your body (avoid hitting your shin. It hurts like a @#$ of a @##$% and leaves a multi-colored mark, mostly black and blue.) and your back leg (the right) will usually follow through into the court. If the toss is behind you or you are not swinging very hard, your right leg may not move at all. As you put more weight shift and effort into your serve, your right leg will naturally follow through into the court (figure 6).

| figure 4 | figure 5 | figure 6 |

The first part of the serve is a leap of faith. We are moving the racket arm with the assumption that the toss arm will do its job. If the toss is a little high, we will wait at the checkpoint. If it's a bit to the left, right, front, or behind, we will make an adjustment. If it is severely flawed, we will catch it or let it bounce, apologize and start over. If it is too low, you will swing at it and probably hit it into the net.

Even though it's too low to hit into the service box, low tosses are almost never caught. You are too rushed to think about whether you should hit it, only thinking about hitting it. **Avoid the low toss. Nothing good can come of it.**

A consistently low toss is like a blind date. As I've said, they are rarely caught, so to hit it successfully we start to swing before we know what's going on, just as a blind date is a commitment to something sight unseen. Yet, since our commitment to the low toss is total, this blind date has dinner **and** breakfast, sight unseen, written all over it. Ouch!

Every serve is a learning experience. If the serve is good, try to repeat it. If it is long, it probably comes from a toss behind you, or not enough wrist to push the racquet face to the correct angle. If it is in the net, the toss is too low at contact (toss might be high enough, just mistimed and struck too low) or too far in front. Occasionally it is from too much wrist, but that's not likely in the beginning. If it is to the left or right of the service box, the racket face was incorrect at contact. This is due to a faulty wrist, grip or toss. This is usually the easiest error to correct.

Power comes from racquet head acceleration, which comes from a loose wrist and the body and arm moving in sync just like a whip. Don't worry. Today's wimpy serve will become tomorrow's weapon as you learn the necessary timing and mechanics.

Most beginners fear the serve most of all because they know that nothing can happen until they get the ball in play. You have never felt pressure until you are serving with three strangers on the court, and you have just double faulted three times in a row.

Line yourself up properly and with a little practice your serve will become consistent. Then we can add speed and spin, and you can start the struggle all over again.

Note: Nowhere in this chapter did I mention bending your knees (will they take away my Tennis Pro card?) or rotating your body. It is not necessary to do either to hit a decent serve. First and foremost it is an arm swing. All the other stuff just complicates things. If you can move your arms while keeping your body quiet, serving will be a snap.

Cindy's Student Notebook

My one fear is not to be able to get my serve in, especially in doubles. I fear everyone is looking at me, like I'm a loser. I didn't use the right grip, but with everything else lined up about right, I got a surprising amount of serves in. They weren't hard, but they were in. Maybe my nine year old son will play with me now. Probably not.

Types of Serves

1. **Flat serve.** Contact is directly behind and through the ball providing maximum speed with very little spin.

2. **Slice serve.** Contact is to the right side of the ball giving it sidespin and making it move from left to right. It is very effective in the deuce court as it can move your opponent off the court opening all kinds of possibilities for you.

3. **Topspin serve.** Contact is low to high along the back of the ball just like a topspin groundstroke. The toss is usually right above your head allowing you to "work" the ball without reaching out and driving right through it.

4. **American Twist or "Kick" serve.** In an American Twist serve the ball jumps up like a topspin serve but "kicks" in the opposite direction of a slice serve. It is a rather difficult serve to hit as the toss is on your left side and puts a lot of strain on your back. Used by better players, it appears more often in the language of veteran players as in "Before I hurt my back I used to have a kick serve that would bounce over your head." Translation: I'm old. I exaggerate.

Common Tennis Terms You Need to Know

Biotch – slang term denoting a person of low moral character as in "That Biotch" called my serve out.

Service Break – If the server wins the service game, he is said to have "held serve." If the service game is lost, it is a service break.

Foot-Fault – Stepping over the baseline or the center line before the serve is struck. Foot-faults are often ignored in casual play and often in league play, depending on the severity of the offense. The problem with calling foot-faults is that the receiver cannot call them, only a line judge can, and in most matches none are available. Often a simple mention to the server will correct the problem as she moves away from the baseline a bit. It also gives the server an excuse for losing (see Biotch) an excuse most avail themselves of.

Chapter 12
The Volley

Tennis has given me soul!
Martina Navratilova

A volley is any ball you hit before it bounces. The only exception is an overhead, and that should be hit about as high as you can reach. Volleys are typically hit closer to the net. If you are closer to the net, you have less time to hit the ball and a faster ball coming at you than if you were standing at the baseline. This presents some problems.

figure 1

- The **grip** is Continental (figure 1). It is Continental for two reasons. We don't have a lot of time for grip changes, and we can use the same grip for both forehand and backhand volley. Secondly, a Continental grip presents an open (to the sky) racquet face which allows us to hit low balls over an ever present net and to hit our volleys with underspin which will keep the ball under control and keep the bounce low. Forehand and backhand grips can be used initially for the volley but only because we are not strong enough yet to use the Continental.

figure 2

- The **Ready Position** (figure 2) is the same as when you are at the baseline. Exception: some players have a two-handed backhand groundstroke but a onehanded backhand volley so their ready position at the net will reflect the one-handed volley, and therefore the left hand will be on the throat of the racquet.

- The **wrist** controls the racquet with the racquet head above the wrist.

- **The contact point** is in front. Because the ball is coming faster and sooner at the net than at the baseline, our backswing will most likely be shorter than at the baseline. How much shorter? Why, **it depends**, of course. The hard hit ball is upon us quickly and has all the energy it needs. Our goal is simply to redirect the ball back to a favorable part of the court without adding any pace. A slower ball allows us more time for a backswing and the need to add some pace, so a bigger backswing is appropriate.

- The **Ideal Volley Position (IVP)** is halfway between the service line and the net. Any closer, and you will be lobbed. Any farther back and most balls are too low and too difficult to hit for winners.

- **Line the ball up as soon as possible.** Lining the ball up early on the volley allows us to do amazing things: sharp angles, clever drop volleys, well placed hard-hit volleys. A good volley begins by taking the racquet *with the correct racquet face* to the anticipated contact point. Do not take it above so you can chop down, nor below, so that you can swing up. If you are at the contact point, you can hit through the ball. What is the correct racquet face? *It depends? Correct!* A low ball requires an open face; an above the shoulder volley may need a closed face. *It depends.*

[If the racquet face for the volley is flat and the ball is lower than the net, the ball will not go over the net. No way. No How. Never.]

Forehand volleys. Try to keep your elbow in as you present your racquet face to the net (similar to the first move on the forehand groundstroke). Keep your elbows forward, and you are more likely to hit the ball in front and less likely to be jammed on balls near your right side. Line up the ball. The backswing is appropriate to the amount of time you have and the pace at which you want to hit the ball. When in doubt, use the shorter backswing. A short backswing means a short follow-through. A bigger backswing requires a bigger follow through. The racquet face should end up facing the target (figures 3, 4, 5).

| figure 3 | figure 4 | figure 5 |

Backhand volleys. Backhand volleys are preferably hit one-handed, but two-handers at the baseline often prefer and/or require two hands at the net. Two-handed backhand volleys, unlike the groundstroke, should be hit with underspin. Extreme backhand grips make this difficult as the face is too closed. Whether one or two handed, try to keep the grip **Continental**. Once again, line the ball up, take an appropriate backswing and keep the strings in line to the target. The arm is **bent–to–straight**. Many two-handers while starting with two hands on the racquet, end with one. This would cause a **bent-to-straight** arm finish.

The one-handed backhand volley, time and skill permitting, is made with the body, upper arm, lower arm, and racquet forming a rectangle (figure 6). Shoulders stay in line to the target, upper arm comes through, lower arm, and then racquet (figure 7). The finish is a **bent-to-straight** arm (figure 8). If time is limited, this rectangle is shortened with just the lower arm and racquet coming through. We don't come to the net to rally. We come to the net to win the point. At the net, you are always looking for an opportunity to end the point.

| figure 6 | figure 7 | figure 8 |

Volleys are safely hit into that part of the court that we can see over the net. From the service line, that means the last third of the court. From the IVP, sharper angles are possible and close to the net, ridiculously sharp angles are possible. Wow your friends and impress the ladies. Of course, if you get too close to the net, you will surely be lobbed and all this will be but a fantasy unfulfilled.

• Grip is Continental

• Line the ball up quickly

• Forehand – keep the elbow forward to start

• Backhand – arm is bent-to-straight

Bob's Student Notebook

I was surprised at how much more time I had on the volley when I didn't change my grip. Of course, most of the time, the racquet magically changed in my hand away from the Continental Grip. I just don't feel strong enough with that grip. As a former power lifter, I can't believe I'm saying that. Little Wendy seems to be doing fine with it, though. Makes me think all those steroids were a waste of time.

Chapter 13
Everything Else

The Lob. You're off the court, barely gotten to the ball, and your opponent is salivating over all the open real estate to hit into. What better plan than to hit the ball high in the air, deep into the court, and return to the middle of the baseline fresh as a daisy and ready to continue?

The **lob**, hitting the ball high into the air to buy some time, is a basic shot in any player's arsenal. There are two types of lobs: defensive and offensive. A defensive lob is used to get you back into the point when other shots have a very small chance of succeeding. An offensive lob is designed to be a winner. The principal difference between them is height. A defensive lob can be hit as high as the ceiling or as high as the sky; in fact, the higher, the better. Offensive lobs are just high enough to clear the outstretched arms of your opponent and horizontal enough to bounce away from him. Since an offensive lob is more precise, it is usually attempted on slightly easier balls. Hard, fast shots hit away from you, or right at you, do not lend themselves to precise replies.

Lobs, like any other stroke, have a backswing, a contact point, and a follow-through (figures 1, 2, 3). The racquet face is open but usually not extremely so. I am always surprised at the players who attempt to lob with a completely open racquet face. If they hit it at all, it flies toward the back fence. A somewhat open racquet face is required. *How open? It depends.* A low, slow ball requires a very open racquet face, while a hard, high ball may only need a face that is slightly open. *It depends.* The faster the ball, the shorter the backswing. The shorter the backswing, the shorter the follow through. Experiment. Attempt to learn from the lob you just hit. Was it too low? too short? too deep? Make an adjustment and try again.

A defensive lob has either no spin or backspin. Spin is often used to convert your opponent's pace into something more manageable. Topspin is rarely used, as it is very hard to take your opponent's hard shot and hit with topspin just over his extended racquet.

figure 1   figure 2   figure 3

An offensive lob can be hit flat, with backspin or with topspin. Why hit it high and deep and let him stay in the point, when you think you can hit just over his head and out of his reach and, if hit with topspin, beyond his ability to retrieve. Flat or underspin offensive lobs are hit the same way as the defensive lob but at a lower angle.

Topspin lobs are not all that different from regular topspin shots. The angle of the racquet face is different to create a higher trajectory. Once again, experiment. The topspin lob does not have to be hit with great topspin. Most errors I see in the shot come from the attempt to hit Federer-like topspin when you don't possess Federer-like topspin. The shot turns into a mishit or a lob that doesn't begin to go over your opponent's head, let alone his outstretched racquet. If you don't try to hit the shot with great pace, you don't need great topspin, and even a little topspin helps pull it down into the court and away from your opponent.

The overhead. Like the bowling ball is to the egg, the natural enemy of the lob is the Overhead. As the name implies, this shot is hit when the ball is over your head. A better definition might be a shot where the ball has an arc, and you have to extend to a straight arm to hit it. Anything else is just a high volley. The motion is similar to the serving motion, so an overhead is simply a serve with someone else tossing the ball, plus you have a lot more court to hit into and you can start from inside the baseline! This should be easy! And it is IF you do these simple things:

1) Turn sideways 90°
2) Point at the ball with your left hand
3) Prepare your racquet, raise your right arm as you raise your left, and drop the racquet head to the backscratch position (don't exaggerate *please*)
4) Keep your feet moving as your left hand struggles to point at the ball and keep it in front of you (figure 4)
5) When the ball is within reach of your racquet – **ATTACK!!!** (figures 5 and 6)

The Overhead is a **confidence** shot, do not chicken out!

| figure 4 | figure 5 | figure 6 |

If you let the ball drop too low, you will miss. If you don't point with the left hand, you will not track it properly and you will miss. If your racquet is down and unprepared, you will be rushed and you will miss. I know that sounds like a lot of ways to miss, but the correct steps are easy enough to do that it's not as hard as it sounds.

Some lobs, particularly outside, are so high that it is very difficult to time as they are dropping so fast. Not to worry, just line yourself up well behind the ball, and let it bounce. As the ball bounces up after it hits the ground, you now line yourself up just as if you're taking it in the air. The important thing is to get back far enough that you can wait for the bounce and then step into the overhead.

As the rubber egg frustrates the mighty bowling ball, so too can a top-spin lob frustrate your mighty overhead. Topspin lobs that bounce over your head are, unfortunately, winners. Topspin lobs that you can reach are dropping faster than normal (remember Bernoulli?). If you are not more aggressive than normal in attacking the ball, the contact point will be **too low,** and you will hit the ball into the net.

In conclusion, **ATTACK, ATTACK, ATTACK!!!!!**

Approach Shots. One of the harder things to do on the tennis court is to make the transition from the baseline to the net. The shot that makes that transition is the **approach shot.** If I had to look at one shot and one shot only to evaluate a player's level, I would choose the approach shot.

The approach shot is not designed to be a winner; it is designed to set up a winning volley. A winning volley is almost always hit from a good volley position: halfway from the net to the service line. To get to that position from the baseline in one shot, two things are neces-sary: 1) your opponent's shot should land short into your court, and 2) you must hit your shot on the run.

Running forward and hitting the ball is difficult. No, make that very difficult. Brushing the ball with a topspin motion is compromised by the fact that your racquet, in addition to brushing the ball, is moving forward as you are moving forward. The minimal topspin you may achieve doesn't help much in keeping the ball in the court, and the topspin bounce sits up perfectly for your opponent's passing shot.

Underspin is the preferred spin for the approach as your racquet can move through the ball without compromising the spin, and the ball stays low, forcing your opponent to hit up to get the ball over the net in a situation where he must hit it hard to get it by you.

That's a problem for him.

The approach shot is a volley hit after the bounce. Early preparation is the key. Most bad approaches are the result of fast feet and slow hands; in our mad dash to get to the ball, we neglect to prepare the racquet. Prepare as if you were hitting a volley with the backswing relatively short as we already have racquet head speed with our feet moving towards the ball. We are hitting the ball in mid-court, so we also have less court to hit into.

Forehand approaches are just running volleys. Backhand approach shots have one more little twist to them. Backhand shots are hit with the front shoulder and, in all cases, are better if the front shoulder stays on line to the target. Running forward and keeping your front shoulder turned towards the net is awkward, if not impossible. Fear not, players smarter than us studied the problem for years and have come up with a satisfactory and somewhat elegant solution (but you're not gonna like it).

figure 7   figure 8   figure 9   figure 10

As you run toward the ball (figure 7), your left foot moves ahead of your right (figure 8) turning your right shoulder toward the net. As you step forward with your right foot, you swing through the ball (figures 9 and 10) keeping your shoulder perpendicular to the net. (I told you you wouldn't like it.) It is actually easier than it looks but it might take a little practice. Just think *right foot, left foot in front, right foot forward and racquet through.*

The quality of your approach determines the difficulty of your volley.

1) Approach shots should, first and foremost, **land in the court**. That may sound stupid, but it's worth mentioning. You are already ahead in this point by virtue of your opponent hitting a short ball. If you don't miss, he will have to hit a passing shot. Some players are terrified at the approach of an onrushing volleyer, others just don't like it. Force the play. If you miss, you let them off the hook.

2) **Depth is important.** By keeping the ball deep you cut down the angles for the passing shot and give yourself more time to react.

3) **Backspin** will keep the ball low, forcing your opponent to hit up.

4) It is noteworthy that **pace**, while helpful, is mentioned last.

Dropshots. Everyone wants to hit a dropshot; to have that ball just drop over the net and leave your opponent flat-footed and in total frustration is truly one of the psychic highs of the game.

Dropshots take some practice but are not extremely difficult.

1) Think of the shot as a lift. This means that we *will not dropshot high balls*. The ball should be at net height or below. Dropshots are best attempted from inside the baseline. Baseline dropshots are very difficult to hit, and they give your opponent much more time to run them down.

2) Backspin is preferred as balls hit vertically with backspin do not want to bounce forward, keeping them closer to the net. Do not chop down on the ball!!!

3) It is not how low it goes over the net, it is where the second bounce occurs. It's not much of a drop shot if the ball goes six inches over the net but crosses the service line before the second bounce.

4) A dropshot is still a stroke, albeit a short one. There is a backswing, contact point, and follow-through (figures 11, 12 and 13). The racquet face is slightly open and the stroke is slightly inverted, creating a little more backspin. The highpoint of the shot is on your side of the net, dropping down as it crosses the net, and with good backspin, bouncing straight up or even backwards forcing your opponent all the way to the net.

| figure 11 | figure 12 | figure 13 |

5) The goal of the dropshot is not to create the unhittable ball; it is to bring your opponent to the net, out of position, and unable to do much with the shot. The real goal is to win the point. With some opponents, just bringing them forward is all you need to do.

6) Touch shots do not come overnight. It takes a little time and work to manipulate that ball on your racquet, but the psychic rewards are much greater than for any other shot. A word of caution: The perfectly placed dropshot is still only worth one point, albeit the only point you'll want to discuss after the match. Do not become too enamored with it.

Bonnie's Student Notebook
My lobs weren't bad, certainly better than my overheads. That's OK. I don't like it at the net anyway. Maybe I can stay at the baseline the whole time. I didn't get the approach shot at all. I kept running up to the ball, hit it, and then back up to the baseline. Drove that instructor guy crazy. Drop shots? Me? Are you kidding?

Common Tennis Terms You Need to Know

Bad Line Caller – Person who calls *good* shots "out" **and** *out* shots "good".

Cheater – Person who calls *good* shots **"out"**.

Line Judge – A person in the wrong place at the wrong time. An individual called upon to officiate (oversee line calls) between two individuals, at least one of whom is a royal pain. Either one player has an overly optimistic view of the placement of his shots, or one player doesn't see the lines particularly well.

Chapter 14
Stroke Problems and Corrections

Luck has nothing to do with it, because I have spent many, many hours, countless hours, on the court working for my one moment in time, not knowing when it would come.
Serena Williams

Human brains being similar for everyone, the mistakes we make on the tennis court are rarely unique. Over the years I have seen a few mistakes for each stroke over and over and over again. I also have discovered the cause and a few solutions for each one. Let's see if you fit any of these descriptions.

Forehands. Error #1 – the "scissors" or the "hug me" forehand. The right arm and shoulder never finishes properly because the left arm and shoulder are going the opposite direction and meet in the middle (figures 1 and 2).

Often the left arm goes in the opposite direction of the backswing and then both arms reverse, colliding in the middle. Something as simple as keeping your left hand on your right side as you take the racquet back may be enough to fix this.

Try putting a racquet in each hand and having them move together through the stroke. The right arm goes back; the left, with the second racquet, does also. They both come through together, left ahead of right with the right hand racquet hitting the ball.

<table>
<tr><td>figure 1</td><td>figure 2</td></tr>
</table>

Error #2 – High-to-low swing (figures 3 and 4). Groundstrokes are a lift. If you do not get under the ball, you cannot lift the ball over the net. Straight backswings tend to go back high and then swing down, similar to a golf shot. Loop backswings, and why would you want anything else?, must drop at the end of the backswing, not as you are coming forward.

figure 3   figure 4

Error #3 – Elbow leads the racquet back (figure 5). I know you'll see Agassi, Nadal, and others doing this, but get real, you are not them. It takes significantly longer to get the racquet into a hitting position this way. Concentrate on getting the *racquet head* back first.

Error #4 – Stance closes, left foot much closer to the sideline than the right. This forces you to hit across your body. Your weight is going to the side, but your racquet is trying to go forward (figure 6). If your first step is a pivot-and-step with your right foot, you will likely end open on your right foot. If the ball is short enough or easy enough, this same pivot and right foot step will allow you to step to the net and not to the side.

figure 5

figure 6

Two-handed Backhand (figure 7). Almost all errors come from doing too much with the left hand and not enough with the right. This sometimes occurs because the right hand grip is too far underneath or just because the left has gone power mad and can't be controlled. Try hitting your backhand with the palm of your left hand against the racquet without wrapping your fingers around the grip. This will force the right to step up and do its job.

figure 7

One-handed backhand. A common error on the backhand is to *open the shoulder* and bring the racquet with it (figure 8), thus not hitting through the shot. Watch Federer's backhand, and you'll see his shoulder perfectly straight, especially when he hits straight down the line. As you swing forward, try sending the left hand in the opposite direction. If the left shoulder won't turn, the right shoulder won't open (they're attached!!!!)

One-handed backhand. Racquet drops below the wrist and is dragged through the shot (figures 9 and 10). Good one-handed backhands have the racquet head even with the wrist for all but the highest balls. Dropping your racquet head below your wrist is not a good substitute for bending the knees to get down for the shot. It is possible to hit a topspin roll from this dropped position, but probably not for you. (I can't do it!)

figure 8   figure 9   figure 10

Serve. Late racquet. The toss arm does not drop with the racquet arm but goes straight up, leaving the racquet arm with an awful lot to do in very little time. (figure 11) The solution is to let the toss arm drop all the way to the front thigh before tossing, allowing both arms to go up together.

Serve. Erratic toss from too much body rotation (figure 12). Hips and shoulder turn as you begin the serve leaving your toss arm at your side and tossing the ball to the side, back, over your head, or worse. Correct by making sure your toss arm stays in line with your left thigh keeping the toss in front and slightly to the right.

figure 11

figure 12

Volley. The most common mistake on the volley is not knowing where the racquet face is and thus mishitting. The initial racquet position, continental grip, racquet head above the wrist at approximately a 45 degree angle can and should be maintained for most volleys. Allowing the racquet head to drop (figure 13) for any ball below the initial racquet face ready position creates all kinds of problems in figuring out where the racquet face is. Of course it has to drop for the lowest of balls but not for just any ball.

figure 13

figure 14 - correct form for low volley

Common Tennis Terms You Need to Know

Easy Match – A match that I won 6-2, 6-2

Close Match – A match that I lost 6-2, 6-2

"Almost every game went to deuce" – A phrase used to describe the closeness of a match that ended 6-0, 6-0, dispelling the notion that it was the massacre the score would indicate.

Hooked, Rooked, Hosed, Jobbed, Jacked, etc., etc. – To lose a match as the result of some questionable line calling by your opponent, as in "I lost 6-0, 6-1, but I was *jobbed*!"

Chapter 15

Safety, Injury and Your Health

I appreciate very much being injury free.
Steffi Graf

If you're hurt, you don't play. If you play, you're not hurt.
Aussie Tennis Code

The easiest way to deal with injuries is to avoid them. *How do I do that, Coach Dave?* Stretching before and after you play will keep your muscles limber and less likely to pull, strain, or tear. When warming up, start slowly, hitting first from the service line, then working your way back to the baseline. I am amazed when I see adults who should know "something" begin playing after less than a minute warming up. I also know that these are not the people who warmed up before they took the court. Hitting more balls in the warm- up allows you to play better, and, therefore, is time well spent. Take at least ten minutes to warm up and at least ten practice serves.

Never, Never, Never when serving, place the second ball near your feet because you don't have pockets. Give the second ball to your partner if playing doubles, give it to your opponent if not, stuff it down your pants if you have to, but never, never put it next to you on the baseline.

If you can avoid running into fixed objects like walls, net posts, and the net, the #1 remaining hazard is the tennis ball lying on your court. The best place for the balls to be is in your pocket. If you are drilling or taking a lesson and have a large number of balls on the court, the safest place for them is at the net. We tend to avoid those dangers we can see, and we should be able to see the balls in front of us. Likewise for the back of the court, for we only get back that far when we turn and run for a lob and, therefore, they are in front of us again. Alert your opponent if balls are close behind him. You shouldn't think the ball on the side of the court is as safe as those at the net. We tend to run to the side far more often than all the way to the net.

> **WARNING:** The most dangerous item on most courts is the metal lid of the tennis ball can you just opened. Handle with care for they are very sharp. The safest place to put it is in the courtside trash caddy or inside the ball can you opened. Keep away from children as they are notorious bleeders.

Despite your best efforts to prevent it, you are probably going to get injured. The body breaks down from repetitive stress. I'm going to talk about the two most common tennis injuries: tennis elbow and plantar fasciitis. I'm not a doctor – at least that's what my paycheck says. Problems with shoulders, backs, knees, and ankles will not be addressed here. Feet and elbow problems are prevalent in the tennis community, and I have seen my share and have a large amount of anecdotal evidence to base my opinions regarding these problems.

Tennis elbow is an inflammation of the epicondylar tendon in the elbow, and it can hurt like a sonof@#$%^#. It's an overuse injury that comes from hitting far more tennis balls than your elbow ever thought it would. It's particularly common among beginner women, women who start to hit a lot of balls after a long layoff, and anyone who hits the ball late. It used to be common among senior women pulling slot machines at the casino, but now that's all push button. No such luck in tennis.

Inflammation injuries usually respond well to ice, anti-inflamma-tory medicines, and rest, and I highly recommend ice, ibuprofen, or naprosyn (Aleve) to help relieve the pain. It has been my experience that rest doesn't usually help. People who have stopped playing be-cause of the pain report taking six months off and within minutes of resuming play find a complete return to their misery. Not all, but most. It's almost as if you have to build up some scar tissue in the elbow before it will go away. Your doctor will probably recommend ice, ibuprofen, and rest, but some are also suggesting that you play through the discomfort. The good news is that it usually does go away and may never reappear. The elbow bands and braces seem to help during play and many players continue to use them to prevent a reoccurrence of the inflammation. The modern lighter, stronger racquets seem to diminish the reoccurrence as well. Once again, this is an observation, not a recommendation, and please remember that I have no medical training whatsoever. Should there be any royalties from this book I don't want them all to go to my lawyer.

Plantar fasciitis is an inflammation of the Plantar fascia ligament that runs from your heel cord through the bottom of your foot. Heel cord stretches, where your foot is firmly placed on the ground as you stretch your calf muscle, help prevent this injury. Because it's your feet, and they are hard to rest completely, plantar fascitis doesn't just go away, and it is very hard to play through. Remember: "No foot, no player!"

The problem is often structural. You have imperfect feet. That was OK when you were 14 and had tendons and ligaments like bungee cords, but it's not so OK now that you are older. Your podiatrist will recommend orthotics, inserts for your shoes that place your feet in a less stressful position. That's no surprise. Your surgeon would probably recommend surgery and your psychiatrist, talk therapy. **The orthotics seem to work.** At least, they seem to work better than anything else I've heard of. Physical therapy and cortisone shots have often been recommended. I would try the orthotics first. Remember this is observation and opinion coupled with absolutely no medical background.

Common Terms You Need to Know

Pusher – 1. A seller of illegal substances, usually drugs. 2. A tennis player whose game consists of relentlessly hitting (pushing?) the ball back, usually without much pace or spin and often with none too pretty strokes. Defeating the pusher is a rite of passage, for it means you did not beat yourself, which is what the pusher relies on. After playing a pusher, some form of medication, often dispensed by the first type of pusher (drugs?) is usually required.

Grinder – A pusher, but with better strokes.

Serve & Volley – Tactic of following your serve into the net hoping to hit a quick winner or to pressure (scare?) your opponent into missing. It is the antithesis of pushing. With only half a court to cover, serve & volley is much more common and effective in doubles.

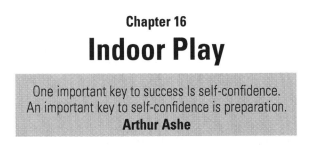

Chapter 16
Indoor Play

> One important key to success Is self-confidence.
> An important key to self-confidence is preparation.
> **Arthur Ashe**

If you play outside tennis year-round, just gloat quietly and move on to the next section. On the other hand, if you play indoors for a portion of the year, here's a few things to keep in mind.

1. You are paying for this court and while YOU may be independently wealthy (you bought my book, didn't you?) the other players on the court may not be, so: Be on time!!!!! I cannot emphasize this enough. Rushing onto court late means that your warm-up time will be reduced, which leads to a slow start which leads to everyone else's game being dragged down to your harried level. Be on time!!!!

2. Be early!!!! Court rates are high, time is short – stretch beforehand.

3. Most indoor court play is set for the entire season. A group of individuals rent the court for the season. You would usually have six people contracting for a doubles court and three or four for singles. If you have a group you would like to play with, great. If not, try to find a group at your level. Remember, this is for the whole year.

4. For those who don't have a group, the club often forms leagues. These leagues allow you to meet new players and play every

week. Some of the leagues are competitive, some are not. Don't be afraid to ask. Try to find a group at your level. I know you don't mind playing against better players. Everyone says that. Better players may mind playing with you, just as you don't want to go out on the court every week and not be challenged because you are too strong for the group.

5. It fascinates me when a group of new players form and say, "We thought we'd play at 7 o'clock Thursday night," as if in the history of the club no one had ever wanted that time. Prime time Monday through Thursday may be tough to get. Find out what is available first.

> The Caste System in India is slowly becoming a thing of the past. The Caste System in tennis is still going as strong as ever, and thus may it always be so. Golfers of widely varying skill can go out and have a good time; unfortunately, not so with tennis players. You need players on a similar skill level to enjoy the game. It's the game's #1 fault.

Indoor groups have a smaller number of players in them. You've played all these people before. You have won some and lost some. Why not practice something in these weekly get-togethers. Today is "come in to the net day," next week is "Don't run around your backhand day" and the week after that is "lob service return day." It might make you better and then next year you'll have to find a different group.

Last, but not least, a tennis community is like a family – a dysfunctional family perhaps, but a family in the sense that they are yours for life. I tell the good young players at the club that there aren't that many of them and that they will be playing with and against each other for a long time. They had better learn to get along. So it is as an adult. The number of players at your level, and available to play when you can play, is not that great. Make friends with all and enemies of none. Diplomacy is one of those skills we won't cover in great detail, but if you don't want to be shut out of the perfect group at the perfect time, play nice.

Chapter 17
Outdoor Play and Practice

*Tennis was never work for me, tennis was fun.
And the tougher the battle and the longer the match, the more fun I had.*
Jimmy Connors

If you live in an area where you can play outside year round, go back and read the section on indoor play. Much of it is relative to outdoor play, and you may have missed a funny line. Before you start gloating about how you can play outside year round and don't have to pay for indoor court time, remember that for at least part of the year, it's hot enough to fry an egg on your courts. With that in mind, here are my thoughts on outdoor play:

1. If you play indoors, you are playing under perfect conditions; No sun, no wind, perfect background, no shadows. There is an adjustment period when you move outside. You will not play as well as you do inside. Even if you do play as well, it won't feel like it. Nothing says "good shot" like a nice echo. Indoors you get one, outside you don't.

2. Outdoor play can be a little more casual. **Be on time anyway!!!** All the reasons for this in the previous section still apply: *lousy warm-up, bad start, etc., drag everyone down.*

3. If it's hot and sunny, wear a hat, use sunscreen, and drink lots of water. No exceptions, none of the time, **not ever.**

4. You probably play more in the outdoor season, so why not use some of that time to work on specific weaknesses and play a few

less matches. At least spend some time (20 minutes) working on a specific skill before you start a set. You never know, that weakness might become a strength (and Bill Gates and I might be related!).

5. If you practice against a wall to improve your stroke, give yourself enough time to feel the stroke and not just react to the ball. The easiest way to do this is to stand farther back and let the ball bounce twice before you hit it. Use the wall to improve your stroke rather than give yourself a workout.

6. Practicing serves. If you wish to practice placement, set a target (a tennis ball can, a bag, a picture of an ex-spouse), step up to that baseline, and fire away. If you hit the target, good for you. If you miss, make an adjustment. In no time your serves will be painting the lines, and you won't be able to count all your aces.

If you wish to practice "serving technique," I suggest you move away from the baseline. If you serve from the baseline, you will judge each serve based on whether it went in the box or not. You'll tell yourself you are just working on power or a specific spin or a better toss, but your brain will judge each and every ball just like an overbearing parent at a Little League game. So, tell yourself anything you want, but move away from the baseline. Move back, or up, and just try to feel the timing and the stroke. When it feels right, move up to the baseline and let that brain judge away.

Are tree limbs and flying birds permanent fixtures, and should you play a "Let" when you hit one? Tree limbs are, flying birds are not, so give yourself a let when that eagle intercepts your lob, but blame the wind for blowing your ball against the branch and costing you the point.

Chapter 18
Fashion

I'm really exciting. I smile a lot, I win a lot, and I'm really sexy.
Serena Williams

Fashion for men consists of two simple rules. Wash your tennis clothes regularly, and by regularly, I don't mean once a season. Secondly, throw out the shirts with holes or big old stains on them. You should not be able to describe your entire tennis career by pointing to various spots on your clothing.

Tip from the wife: half a cup of ammonia in the wash will make those sweaty clothes smell much better.

Fashion for women. Ladies, can we talk? There is really only one issue in women's tennis fashion and that is the **tennis skirt!** Unless you are considering wearing one of those very skimpy shorts outfits that the 19 year old female pros are wearing (and who is considering that?), the tennis skirt is the issue.

There are two schools of thought to be discussed here. The first is: "I can't wear a tennis skirt because I stink as a player. I can't go out there looking like I know what I'm doing and then hit the ball all over the building. It's sweatpants for me until my confidence level gets to where I think I look like I belong out here."

I disagree. If you dress like a hooker, people will think you are a hooker. If you dress in a tennis skirt, people will still want to see you hit the ball before they decide if you are a player or not. If not, no false advertising claims have been made.

The second school of thought is: "I will never wear a tennis skirt. My legs are not for public viewing." While this is constitutionally permitted under the "pursuit of happiness" clause, it gets awfully hot on court at least some of the time.

If you don't go with the skirt, you are going to have to go with the shorts, (No, not those tiny shorts outfits mentioned above, but if you look good in those, send me a picture.) because sweatpants just will not cut it year 'round.

One common question is "Where do I put the second ball when I am serving?" Many tennis skirts have compression shorts built right into them and the second ball fits neatly underneath them. Some of the compression shorts even have pockets for balls, but I hear you have to dig around way too much to get them out. Never having dug the ball out myself, I'll take the word of my experienced female players. Most shorts have pockets, at least all the ones you'll be wearing. There are even little plastic ball clips that attach to the waistband that neatly hold a tennis ball. If you do wear sweatpants or warm-up pants, be sure that there is a pocket.

It has been my experience that looking good often helps you to play better. Something about positive self image or self esteem seems to be at play, but I believe it to be true.

In conclusion, wear something comfortable – comfortable in the way you look, comfortable in the way you feel. Anything else takes away from the fun you are supposed to be having.

Four young girls ages 11-13 called me for some beginner lessons. After an hour and a half of constant hitting and instruction and silence from the girls, I asked if they had any questions. The youngest was the only one to speak, and the only question was, "Do you know where I can get one of those tennis skirts?"

EXTREME FASHION

My friend Jerry had a chance to play the living legend, Dr. Bob Something-orother, in the finals of the prestigious West Virginia Open 35 and over tournament. Dr. Bob had won the Open Division and the 35 numerous times and was the favorite again even though he was 45. He came out wearing a back brace, an elbow brace, and two knee braces and still managed to beat Jerry in three long sets. Jerry's post match assessment was a simple one. "I could have beaten him if we were both naked! But nobody would have watched!"

Pressure comes in many forms. One lowly ranked professional trying to make his way on tour without a sponsor related this comparison: If you think there is pressure playing in the finals of a Grand Slam tournament in front of thousands for millions of dollars, try playing a tournament in Libya knowing that if you do not win this match, you won't have enough money to leave the country!

A satellite player who had just won three consecutive matches by a score of 7-5 or 7-6 in the third set explained why he wasn't nervous in those situations. "Years ago I was in a third set tiebreaker and down 6-0. I won four consecutive points before losing the next point and the match. As we were shaking hands at the net I noticed his hands were wet and shaking. I realized he was far more nervous about losing a tiebreaker after being up 6-0 than I was being down 6-0 and since then I have assumed in those situations that my opponent is probably more nervous than I am and with that knowledge (true or otherwise), I usually play very confidently and relaxed in those situations. I don't always win, but I think I am going to."

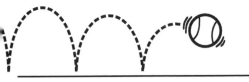

Chapter 19

USTA Leagues

> You win some...you lose some.
> Nothing wrong with that.
> **Stefan Edberg**

Many years ago the USTA (United States Tennis Association) came out with the NTRP (National Tennis Rating somethingorother). It created a rating system for players more specific than beginner, intermediate, and advanced. The system describes players from 1.0 (total beginner) to 7.0 (Andy freakin Roddick) in 0.5 point increments.

Leagues were then formed with the idea of placing players of equal skill in a competitive situation. Most areas have leagues from 2.5 to 5.0, with the majority of players being in the 3.0 – 3.5 range.

Teams usually consist of about 12 players competing in a two singles, three doubles match format once a week. Eight players are needed each week giving each player some leeway to have a life other than tennis during the season.

There are leagues for men, women, seniors (over 50), super seniors (over 60), and mixed doubles. Minimum age is usually 19. The season is spring and summer, with regional, sectional, and even national championships. A super computer similar to HAL (2001: A Space Odyssey) and just as warped is used to determine new player ratings for the next season.

Players may play up a level; that is, a 3.0 may play at the 3.5 level, but players cannot play below their level. If all your friends are on a

3.5 team and you are only rated 3.0, you may still be able to play on their team (if they'll have you).

So now you know what USTA League tennis is. Here's what you really need to know.

There are two kinds of USTA teams, competitive teams and fun teams. Competitive teams would like to win their league, win sectionals, win nationals, and go to Disney World. Fun teams enjoy playing every week (they are still competitive players) and socializing afterwards. Some teams are both. You may be very competitive at the 3.5 level, win the league, do well regionally, have most of your players move up to 4.0, and suddenly be one of the fun teams that aren't (can't be) so competitive at 4.0.

Some teams practice regularly. Some don't. Some practice with a coach. Some don't. Most teams will play you just as much as anyone else on the team. Some teams are going to play their best players a lot more. Some teams bring great snacks for afterwards (women); some have a bag of chips and beer (men).

Being captain of a team is fun. You get to organize who's on the team. You get to make the match lineup deciding who gets to play and with whom. You get to adjust the match lineup when Bernie or Brigitte call on match day and tell you they forgot that they had a previous engagement. (A closer analysis of Brigitte and Bernie's last-minute cancellations might suggest some kind of extracurricular activities unrelated to tennis, but that is beyond the scope of this text.)

As captain, you get special attention from your teammates. They love to call and offer helpful advice on who should play and with whom and why.

Some people love to be captain, type "A" personalities mostly, and some do an excellent job year in and year out. Some like to be captain just to make sure they are in the lineup each week. Many teams rotate the captaincy each year to share the pain. **Be kind to the team captain.**

A series of questions should be forming in your head regarding USTA Leagues before you decide to play on a team.

1. What level am I? There is a self-rating questionnaire provided by the USTA before you register, but I suggest you ask a pro familiar with your game instead.

2. Do I want to be on a "competitive" team or a "fun" team?

3. Do I want to have regular practices with or without a pro?

4. Do I want to play singles, doubles, both, or whatever the team needs?

5. How many people are on the team. Some teams have 15 or 16 people – more people, fewer matches per person.

It is always flattering to be asked to join a team. My suggestion is to ask a few questions before you jump in and accept the first offer.

If you are new to everything and don't know who to talk to about getting on a team, the USTA website (USTA.com) will refer you to the local league coordinator who can then refer you to a team looking for players.

Joining a team is not like getting married. It's more like dating. Some dates work out. Some don't. Players join and leave teams (after the season) all the time and for a wide variety of reasons. Some players get moved up in rating, some players have personality conflicts (I know it's hard to believe, but it happens). Some just want to play on a team that is more/less competitive or that practice closer to home or who knows what else. Some teams stay pretty much intact year in and year out.

Lastly, if you hang around tennis players a little bit, you will hear some USTA horror stories – Bitchy women, men in fistfights, atrocious line calling, and even worse. These incidents are the exceptions. I believe that overall, the good far outweighs the bad. I'm not sure, but league participation may be at an all-time high. Try it. You might like it.

> When you are very little, tennis should be fun, it should be a game.
> **Guy Forget**

> When you are an adult in a league, tennis is all about the wins and losses.
> **Dave Kocak**

> Victory is fleeting. Losing is forever!
> **Billie Jean King**

Chapter 20
"A Tale of Two Ladies"

DONNA

I finally decided to take up tennis. It's something I've always wanted to do and now I'm finally doing it. Jim thinks I need a break from just being a Mom, and the exercise will do me good. It's only $100 for the eight weeks. I didn't have the courage to do it myself so I got my friends Sue, Jeanie, and Monica to join me. They said they haven't played in years and didn't play much then. They really don't consider themselves any more than beginners like me. First class is next week. I CAN'T WAIT!

MONICA

Donna asked me to join her beginner tennis group. I haven't played since high school and I wasn't very good then. She made it sound like a lot of fun, and it should be good exercise. I just hope I don't embarrass myself. I don't know Jeanie and Sue but Donna says they are real nice.

DONNA – WEEK ONE

The pro's name is Jean-Pierre. I think he is French-Canadian. Kinda cute with a French accent to boot. He laughed a little at Jim's old racquet, telling me it was too heavy and the grip was too big. He gave me a demo to try. There's just the four of us in the class which is nice, lots of personal attention. I must admit it is a lot harder than I imagined. I even swung and missed at several balls. Jean-Pierre was very encouraging as were all the girls. Sue, Jeanie, and Monica were hitting the ball pretty good for not having played in years. Jean-Pierre

89

was kinda impressed with them and told me it would be good to be in this class as they would help me improve faster.

MONICA – WEEK ONE
I thought I did pretty well for not having played in years. It felt great to hit the ball again. Jean-Pierre, the pro, said I have real good wrist control and a natural forehand. He said my racquet was too heavy, and he gave me a demo to use. Much lighter and I hit much better. Jeanie and Sue are very nice and they hit very well. We all tried to encourage Donna because we know how hard it is in the beginning.

DONNA – WEEK TWO
I couldn't wait to get back on the court and hit the ball again. I'd hoped it would be better than last time, but it seemed about the same. There's so much to remember, and by the time I try to stroke the ball it's already on top of me. J.P. says I need to control the racquet with my wrist, but since I've never done this before, my wrist is weak. Jeanie showed up in a real cute tennis outfit she just bought. I want to be good enough to feel like I can wear those tennis skirts instead of sweatpants. All the other girls are doing real well, and they are giving me lots of positive reinforcement.

MONICA – WEEK TWO
Couldn't wait to get back on court and hit the ball again. Felt even better than last time. I think I'm getting my timing back. J.P. wants me to try to start hitting with topspin on my groundstrokes. Jeanie showed up in a tennis outfit. Looks great on her. Wonder where she got it. I really like her and Sue. I'm so glad Donna talked me into this.

DONNA – WEEK THREE
What the hell is topspin? The other girls are using it. Hey, it's not like I knew where the ball was going to bounce before, but with this spin stuff I am totally baffled. J.P. says I will figure it out and not to worry, but he doesn't sound sincere. Maybe it's just that phony French-Canadian accent. Now all the girls have new tennis outfits, and I still

have my sweats. I thought this was going to be a nice recreational thing. Oh, and then a new girl was added to the group, Amy. I'll tell you one thing – she ain't no beginner. I'm starting to feel a twinge in my elbow.

MONICA – WEEK THREE

I am just loving this tennis class. Now I'm hitting with topspin on both my forehand and backhand! So are Jeanie and Sue. Donna is still struggling. She's trying real hard, but she has a long way to go. I hope she stays positive. Wore my new tennis outfit today. All this exercise is making me lose weight or at least firm up. I feel great. We added a new girl to the group, Amy, who hits great.

DONNA – WEEK FOUR

We learned how to volley today. J.P. fed us balls while we were much closer to the net, and we hit them in the air. Finally, something I was OK at. All you had to do was stick your racquet out and step to the ball. Maybe I'll get this after all. :-) Jim says I've been miserable for days after my lesson. Maybe I'll make him his favorite meal tonight! I don't think I like Amy, not sure why. Girls all had on different outfits than last week. Better go shopping, already two outfits behind. Did notice when I hit the ball off center that I got a big pain in my elbow. J.P says to put a little ice on it when I finish playing.

MONICA – WEEK FOUR

Today was volley day. J.P. fed us lots of balls nice and slowly so that we could get the technique right. At least, that's what he said. I think he did it that way so Donna would actually hit some balls. Amy suggested that Sue, Jeanie, and I could get together and play some doubles this week. Sounds great.

DONNA – WEEK FIVE

J&*% C$#%$, my elbow hurts. Did everything lefthanded all week. Thought about not coming this week but wanted to build on my volley success last week. This week J.P. put two players on the baseline and two players at the net. I wasn't very good at the baseline but couldn't wait to get to the net. I never realized how hard those girls hit the ball. When I wasn't swinging wildly and missing, I was ducking or getting hit with the ball. And when I hit the ball off center the pain was so bad I just wanted to sit down on the court and cry like a baby. J.P. said to put something cold on it when I finished. I chose a quart of chunky chocolate ice cream.

MONICA – WEEK FIVE
Lost another pound this week and also feel a lot fitter. Played doubles with Sue, Amy, and Jeanie this week and we just had a great time together. Felt bad when I hit Donna with the ball during a volley drill. I didn't think I hit it that hard. Playing again this week with Amy, Sue, and Jeanie. We decided not to tell Donna, thought it might hurt her feelings.

DONNA – WEEK SIX
Taking 800 mg of ibuprofen 4 times a day, and I still can't turn a doorknob with my right hand. What the hell am I doing here? Overheard the girls talking about their tennis game this week. Thanks for inviting me!!! We started serving today and, as usual, the four princesses were doing just fine as I was tossing the ball all over the court. Forget about hitting it, I couldn't even toss it somewhere I could reach it. Jim suggested I get a new racquet. J.P. says the $79 or $99 one will do, but you know, I do hit better with that $200 model.

MONICA – WEEK SIX
Thought Donna might not come today since her elbow hurts so bad, but she toughed it out. I never knew she swore so much and so creatively. Farm animals making love is the best way to describe it. Anyway, I was hoping we could do some more advanced stuff with her gone. She's still my friend, but she's like the black hole of tennis. The ball comes to her but it never comes back. I think she overheard us talking about our doubles this week. I hope I didn't hurt her feelings, but she must realize she's in the wrong class.

DONNA – WEEK SEVEN
No longer feel the pain in my elbow. Of course I no longer feel my hand or my fingers either. Tried to get some help with my serve but

Silicone Suzie was monopolizing J.P. How does she hit a backhand with those things anyway? Didn't tell Jim about my $200 racquet. I just make sure there's extra cash coming back when I write the check for groceries at the market. J.P. ended by telling me I was much improved. He said some other shit too.

MONICA – WEEK SEVEN

The four of us talked about getting regular court time after the lessons are through. J.P. had some league suggestions and showed us which clinics we could take. Wish I had started this earlier. I feel ten years younger. Not sure which racquet to buy. I feel like I hit pretty well with all of them.

DONNA – WEEK EIGHT

Played doubles this week. I don't know where to stand. Don't know how to keep score. This Deuce-Ad thing is so confusing and what math illiterate designed the 15-30-40?? scoring. Despite all that, I finally hit some good shots. Of course those bitches called them out. Somebody should tell them the lines are "IN"!!

MONICA – WEEK EIGHT

Donna was a little late today. I hope she didn't notice our "under the breath" moans as we saw her walk on the court. We all played doubles today and Donna surprisingly hit a few good shots. Unfortunately, most of them were a few inches out. Some ladies who have been watching us play asked us to join their USTA team. We're delighted to be able to stay together. Can't wait to wear my latest outfit and try out my new racket!!!

EPILOGUE

When asked by J.P. to sign up for another group of lessons and join the USTA beginners league, Donna's reply was, "Absolutely. You know me. I just love Tennis!

The WCT (World Championship Tennis) circuit was one of the first U.S. pro circuits. The money was paltry compared to today's prize money, and many of the lesser players struggled to make ends meet. Often, the elites of the tennis community in the host city would house the players during the tournament. The host family would usually meet the player at the airport in a Lincoln, Mercedes or whatever they had lying around at home. An Australian Doubles player was met by a rather striking young lady in a Volkswagen Beetle. Upon arrival at her modest house he was informed that there was only one bed, and would he mind sharing? A consistent first round singles loser, he made it to the singles final and won the doubles. Chalk one up for Volkswagen!

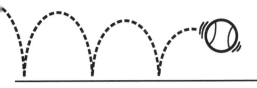

Chapter 21
The Good Student

If you don't practice, you don't deserve to win.
Andre Agassi

The worst tennis lesson of my life occurred in my first Country Club job when I was young and foolish. A high-powered malpractice attorney wanted a forehand lesson. He said his backhand was fine, but his forehand needed some work. After feeding a few balls I was feeling great. His backhand was fine, but his forehand was atrocious and I, Dave Kocak, tennis pro extraordinaire, knew why. He was trying to hit a forehand with a backhand grip, a most difficult thing to do. You have to raise your elbow into an awkward position, high balls are nearly impossible, balls sail all over the place, etc., etc.

I stopped hitting and proudly exclaimed that I knew what was wrong with his forehand and that I could fix it. "All you have to do," I said, "was change your grip. Just move the racquet in your hand an inch or so to a forehand grip, and you'll be fine by the end of the lesson." *(Even way back then I was such a smart fellow!)*

Mr. Attorney informed me that he couldn't change his grip. I explained it was just a simple turn of the racquet by the opposite hand. Didn't matter. He couldn't do it, **and** he didn't want to try.

All I remember about the rest of that lesson was being quiet and feeding balls. Twenty eight years later and I still remember.

He was not a good student.

A good student is punctual. I feel compelled to give you an hour lesson, if possible, even if you are 15 minutes late and it screws up my lunch. Not all pros feel this way and since it's your money.......

There are no dumb questions if **you** don't know the answer. Sometimes pros assume too much.

Good pros usually don't talk much more than a minute at a time. If you are in a group lesson, avoid making the pro repeat himself or give you that *"First Grade Teacher Stare"* that shut you up and made you put your head down on your desk in shame.

Be open to new ideas and be willing to work on it a bit before announcing "I can't do it that way!" That's what your eight year old does.

Grip changes are difficult, (it's amazing how turning your hand a little bit on the racquet is like giving up your favorite security blanket) but sometimes necessary. The earlier in your career you begin using the right grip, the less traumatic the change will be.

You didn't come to the lesson to tell the pro what's wrong with your game. You came to the lesson to let the pro fix your game. Don't tell her "my backswing is too big" or "I have a hitch in my serve." Let the pro evaluate. Maybe, just maybe, she can tell you **why** your backswing is too big or **why** you have a hitch in your serve, and more importantly, how to fix it.

Good students **practice!** They practice against the wall, with a friend, in front of the mirror, or at the office, but they practice. And because of that, they get better.

Chapter 22

Maximizing Your Instructional $$$

The difference between involvement and commitment is like ham and eggs.
The chicken is involved, the pig is committed.
M. Navratilova

If you are like most of the people I teach, your time and / or your financial resources are limited. *(Sorry, Dave, I don't think "limited" states the case strongly enough.)* How to get the biggest bang for the buck is your concern, isn't it? I thought so.

Tennis instruction comes in three forms: private lessons, group lessons, and drill clinics.

Private Lessons: Private lessons are the best way to learn to play tennis. With only one student to worry about, the pro can spend the appropriate amount of time on each aspect of your game. If you have a good forehand but no backhand, you can concentrate on improving that stroke exclusively, taking the time to learn it the "right" way. In a private lesson you hit all the balls, allowing you more opportunities to hit it correctly and grooving in your stroke. What could be better? Hitting with the pro is preferable to hitting with someone at your level in other ways. Think of him or her as **"Goldilocks."** The pro gives you the perfect ball to hit; not too hard, not too soft, but just right. Enough spin but not too much with placement just challenging enough.

"That sounds great, Dave, but what's it going to cost me?"

Private lessons from a competent professional vary a great deal. If you live in Beverly Hills it will cost you more than if you live in Smallville, but even in Smallville a one-hour outdoor private lesson should be $30 or more. Indoor lessons will be more, and remember, you don't live in Smallville.

Group Lessons: Group lessons are obviously less expensive than private lessons, and there are some drawbacks, but don't feel that Richie Rich or his sister (what is her name?) will automatically improve faster than you. Depending on your current level, a group lesson may be just as good as a private lesson. If you are a beginner who needs information, that information can just as easily be imparted to three, four, or five people as easily as to one. If your group is here to learn the proper grip, stroke, positioning, and strategy, that knowledge is just as easily disseminated to a group as to an individual. A good group lesson will still have you hitting lots of balls and getting lots of personal instruction, perhaps not quite as much as a private lesson, but still quite a bit. A bad group lesson will have you hitting one ball and going to the end of the line awaiting your....... turn....to.....hit ....one........ball.........again. Avoid these.

Drill Clinics: Drill clinics are an excellent way to practice what you have learned. Drill clinics are pro-supervised sessions where through a series of drills and games, you can practice all aspects of your game. Different clubs do these in different ways. Some clinics are designated for a specific skill level, others have multiple pros and the whole range of levels. Some are drop in, pay as you go; some are group packages. Check to see how your club or pro does it.

Most drill clinics consist of a good warm-up followed by drills designed to emphasize one specific part of the game. It might be groundstrokes today, volleys next week, lobs and overheads another, and doubles strategy the following class. Usually you end up playing some kind of competitive singles or doubles at the end.

In a good clinic you should receive some helpful criticism from the pro, lots of hitting with a variety of players, and the opportunity to practice in a game situation.

Clinics usually run longer (1½ - 2 hours) and cost less than either private or group lessons. The groups are often larger than lesson groups and rely more on the pro to structure the drills and offer advice while de-emphasizing pro ball feeding. When deciding which clinic to attend, be realistic in your evaluation of your game. *"I don't mind playing up"* is heard far too often. You don't mind playing up, but the other people mind playing down to you. If you are unsure, ask the pro. He'll be happy to give you a 30 second evaluation; after all, he doesn't want you in the wrong group either.

Instruction can be done in a group or a drill. Corrections, particularly with a mature, grooved stroke usually require a fair amount of time and individual attention. Change is hard!

Private lessons will get you where you want to go the fastest. "Good" group lessons can be more cost effective. Drill clinics to reinforce what you have learned. Match play will prove if any of it stuck!

Tennis Pro Conundrum: Multiple critiques and repeated corrections give one the feeling of "being picked on." Very few corrections leave you feeling ignored. If you receive multiple criticisms from your pro, repeated over and over, that is called "Special Attention" and it is to be cherished.

My friend Brian was in high school playing someone who, although not a great player, was undefeated except for two losses to Brian. The third match found Brian down match point. His opponent served, Brian returned it to the middle of the court and his opponent proceeded to call the ball "Out" and ran off the court in victory. Brian followed to protest the call. The officials asked if he now wanted a line judge. When informed that the disputed call was match point they said there was nothing they could do.

I watched young Mike begin a tournament match against a similar type player. I didn't see much beyond the first game but both kids could stroke the ball quite well. I saw Mike after the match and asked for the score. The reply was "He won 6-2, 6-2, but he's not better than me!" My guess is that he thinks that he is!

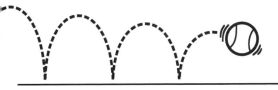

Chapter 23

Tennis Pros

"You see that fellow over there, laddie? He couldn't train Lassie to Bark!"
**Overheard in Fort Erie Racetrack infield regarding a horse trainer.
Unfortunately, often appropriate at the tennis club.**

In the not-so-distant past the term "Tennis Professional" was attached to anyone who was able to convince someone or several someones to pay them money to instruct them in the game of tennis. There were few, if any, professional guidelines, qualifications, or accreditations regarding the teaching of the game. The USPTA (United States Professional Tennis Association) had a rating test for its members, but it was mostly a skills test with very little emphasis on the teaching aspect of the game.

That was then. This is now. The USPTA now has a more rigorous test for its teaching pros. This was at least in part prompted by the rival PTR (Professional Tennis Registry), which placed far more emphasis on teaching and less on playing ability. The result is that there are far more competent tennis instructors today than 30 years ago.

That's the good news. The bad news is that professional accreditation is no guarantee of competence. It should be, but it's not, and without some experience or some reference points, you probably won't be able to tell the difference. For any one of a number of reasons, far too many pros fit far too many criteria in my top ten chart at the end of this section. They may lack enthusiasm after too many years doing the same thing. (It's important that the students aren't bored. It's just as important that the teacher isn't bored.) They may not possess the technical skills needed to assess and correct stroke mechanics or the people and language skills needed to pass that information along. Too many people think they want to teach tennis because they like to play tennis. The two are very different. Teaching has also been a landing place for good high school or college players who didn't know what else to do with their lives.

More good news. Most clubs with two or more teaching pros have one or more competent ones. The trick is to recognize who they are and get them on your court or with your children.

The usual procedure at most clubs is that the best players get the best teachers. This may actually be the reverse of what makes the most sense but nevertheless is the usual status quo. The top players, certainly the top junior players, are spending more money at the club than the beginner or casual player and, therefore, get more attention from the Tennis Director or the Head Pro. Besides, the technical skills needed to improve already very good players may require the club's best pro. This does not mean that beginners should be left with whatever or whomever is available. Unfortunately, they often are.

WARNING: If you are a beginner, talented or otherwise, and you take lessons, you will improve. It is hard not to. If you are talented or have lots of sports-related experience, you may improve rapidly. You will attribute much of this rapid improvement to your teacher, deserving or not. If you are inexperienced with ball sports and untalented besides, you will still improve. Perhaps not as fast as you would like, but improve you will. Everyone does. And, great news for your instructor, you will probably attribute your too slow improvement entirely to your lack of skill and experience rather than his. It's a "can't lose" for the pro.

So, how can I tell if my instructor is competent? The top ten list at the end of this section is a humorous look at the problem, but here is what good pros look for in the work of their colleagues.

Number 1 is *stroke production.* Does the student stroke the ball better than when they started? Remember, you will hit more balls in play than when you started as a result of practice, improved timing, ball sense, and reflexes, but real improvement is tied to improved technique.

Number 2 is *efficient use of time.* Are the drills helpful and appropriate? In a group lesson, is there a better way to get more players hitting more balls in an effective manner? This addresses everything from efficient ball pickup to games and drills that the class can benefit from.

Number 3 is *the lack of emphasis* on very basic information or the transmission of incorrect information. For example: after one lesson with me you might not return to the "ready position" after each and every shot, but you know damn well you should and that I'll mention it if you don't.

Number 4 is *the tolerance of glaring errors.* An extreme example would be "hands reversed on a two-handed backhand" or an extremely inappropriate grip for the intended shot.

I realize that most students don't have the knowledge to analyze their instructor properly, which is what I said at the beginning of this chapter. Now you know a little more. To my fellow pros: Don't take the list too seriously, but don't resemble it, either.

TOP TEN SIGNS YOUR TENNIS PRO MAY NOT BE THE BEST

#10. He has one hopper of half-dead balls for 10 students

#9. Each drill is hit one ball, go to the end of the line

#8. After five weeks he still calls your kids "Buddy" and "Sweetie"

#7. Every ball that goes in is a **"Nice Shot"**

#6. Every ball that doesn't go in is because you didn't **"Watch the ball"**

#5. While every lesson has elements of review, he teaches the **SAME** lesson every week

#4. Spend as much time picking up balls as hitting them

#3. When he does play in your drill or game, loves to show off by hitting winners

#2. Has to take at least one "important" cell phone call each lesson

And the #1 reason your pro may not be the best:
Lassie doesn't bark!!!

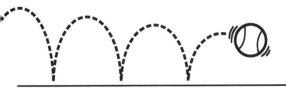

Chapter 24
Tennis For Kids

We don't know who we are until we see what we can do.
Martha Grimes

Just like most of the answers to stroke questions, the answer for kids and tennis is often "It depends." "What's the right age to start?" "How many days a week should she play?" "Should I put my children in the same group?" All these questions have "It depends" kind of answers. Hopefully my thoughts and observations on the subject will help you make intelligent decisions for your child. I wish I had talked to someone about it, for although I was a lifelong tennis pro, I was a first time parent.

4-6 year olds. Americans love to get out in front and start their kids in sports as early as possible. That's what the other kids on the street are doing so there may be no alternative. Most kids who take tennis at this age are probably playing soccer, maybe T-Ball, and swimming. All these things are easier to learn than tennis. Remember, **Ball Sense and Racquet Skills.**

If you have played catch with your child or thrown tennis balls at him, he may have developed some ball sense. She also may be a good little athlete who has good hand-eye coordination. Hitting tennis balls may be fun, especially if the child is good at it. Technique is not particularly important yet, but enjoying the experience is. There is not much a pro can do at this point that a parent cannot, particularly if you follow the advice below.

Your child hasn't played catch or had tennis balls thrown at her, and his athleticism at this age is somewhat suspect. What do I do? You should be your child's first tennis pro, and you can be if you follow these simple steps.

1. No age is too young for tennis if you and your child are having fun, although 2½ - 3 years old would seem to be the lower limit.

2. Get a bunch of tennis balls, preferably not too lively. Your old ones, or the new USTA low pressure ones are good.

3. Instruction consists of "One hand on the forehand and two hands on the backhand," and even that is negotiable.

4. The minimum distance for you to toss to your child should be from service line to baseline. Even if you move your child closer to the net because he is young and small, try to maintain this distance. If you are too close, she doesn't have time to track the ball and develop some ball sense.

5. The ideal toss is a ball that bounces several feet in front and then drops into their hitting zone. Hitting on the rise is a learned skill for adults; think how hard it will be for your little darling. Try to create some movement by tossing a few feet to either side occasionally.

6. Move them as close to the baseline as you can get them and still have them hit it over the net.

7. Use the largest racquet that they can maneuver. This might be a racquet-ball racquet, a peewee tennis racquet, or something larger.

8. Make up some game that your child can win. It's OK if they don't win all the time. Avoid making "in your face" taunts if they should lose!

9. If he cries, you're done. If you cry, well, maybe this wasn't such a good idea after all.

10. There are four sizes of tennis racquets.

    A. Full size (27-28½ inches)

    B. 26 inches

    C. 25 inches

    D. Too small to be paying for "private" lessons

7-9 year olds. By this age your child has shown some interest in sports or not. You have some idea of their athletic inclinations and abilities. He may have hit some tennis balls or he may be a total beginner. Things to pay attention to:

1. **The Group is very Important.** Children need to fit into the group on the tennis level and the social level. If your child is a little boy who can hit the ball, he may not like being in with a group of older girls, even if they can hit the ball. If he's in with boys who can't hit, the parent expresses reservations because he is "not being challenged enough." You need to find a balance.

2. The racquet should be the **largest** they can handle. You will see, at first, a struggle to deal with the larger racquet, followed by an improved stroke pattern and more power. Racquets that are too small tend to allow for extremely whippy strokes that don't do anyone any good. Very young children struggle with larger racquets as much for the grip as for the weight. Those little hands have a hard time reaching around even a 4 1/8" grip. Flying racquets on forehands and serves are not uncommon.

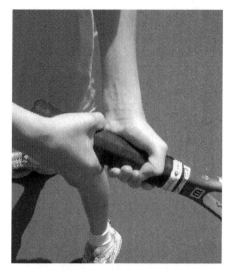

small hand, big grip   better with two hands

3. Whether in a group or hitting with a parent, it's time to put some emphasis on technique. Proper technique will also force your child to use his wrist properly, developing the wrist strength that is so important for tennis. Forehand and service grips may be a little extreme to compensate for weak arms and wrists.

good technique possible, even with a little guy

4. **A good pro is a plus.** Hitting a lot of balls at the right speed from the right distance with the proper emphasis on form is very important. He should be likeable also.

5. **Have fun!** If it's not fun, now may not be the time for tennis. Back off, man! It's "A sport for a lifetime!" so what's the rush?

Older beginners

Older kids don't like being with younger kids, particularly if the younger kids are better. No 5'9" 15 year old girl wants to be embarrassed by some tiny little ten year old boy. Social level is far more important than skill level for this group. It would be nice to have a junior novice class for these kids. Many clubs do.

At some point between the ages of 4 and 9 you discovered that your kid is a very good athlete. You are not alone in this realization. At least one tennis coach has spotted him/her and will tell you that your child has a future in tennis and this may very well be true. Don't get too excited. The baseball, basketball, football, soccer, and hockey coaches will probably tell you the same thing, and this may also be true. Be careful about specializing too young.

In the System

Your child has taken several group sessions, maybe a few private lessons, plays in a junior league and/or has played a few tournaments. Your kid is now a tennis player. You are "**In the System.**"

Your first questions should be: "Who's looking out for me?" Who is my advocate in the system? Who will tell me if my child needs a different racquet? That he needs a better lesson group? That he should play in this league? Or in that tournament? Who?

By now you've spent a few dollars and you are likely to spend many more. If I assume you are not well acquainted with junior tennis and how this all works, you need someone who is. He should be the pro who is teaching your child. If it's not him, why is he teaching your child? If not him, then the head pro.

The Tennis Brat

You probably have a very nice child, perhaps even more than one. He/she gets along with other children, is polite around adults and even has a pretty good sense of humor.

He might be a little bit spoiled, but whose kids aren't in this day and age? If this is true, and I'm guessing that for most of you it is, I am also guessing that you have a question for me. It probably goes something like this: **"How come I don't recognize my kid on the tennis court?"** I see behavior ranging from obnoxious to embarrassing, from unsportsmanlike to outright cheating. What's going on?"

Before I answer that I'd like to give you a little personal background. I played baseball from the age of nine and basketball from the age of 11, and I was good. Even though I was good, I failed a lot. Fortunately, it was never my fault. The umpires, the referees, and even occasionally my teammates were to blame. *"Still perfect after all these years!"*

> It's about you. It's you if you win. It's you if you lose.
> Black and White. Nowhere to hide.
> **Greg Rusedski**

Your child is out on the tennis court all by himself, and if the match is close, he's failing a lot. Close to 50% of the points are going to his opponent. And just like me, he's looking for someone else to blame. But unlike me, he can't find that someone, and that's a big dilemma for a young person who has invested so much time, energy, and ego into an endeavor. "Maybe I can blame the other player." "I can't believe he could call that ball out." "I wanted it to be on the line and I'm sure that it was." "I want to win so bad that it seems unfair that it's not happening." **"I don't know how to deal with this!"**

I do not condone bad behavior on the tennis court. I've pulled kids off the court in the middle of a match. I've sat kids down in lessons. I've suspended kids from the club.

I do not condone bad behavior on the tennis court, but *I understand it*. I never played as a junior so I've never experienced it, but I think I understand it. Now you do, too.

There is good news. Most kids learn how to deal with the pressure; most of those who don't get tired of embarrassing themselves and switch sports. The bad news is that a few never learn how to control their emotions (insert John McEnroe video here), and some even continue to be obnoxious as adults.

If your kid hasn't gotten himself under control, I'm not sure what the solution is. Bjorn Borg's parents took his racquets away for six months, and he was the "stoic Swede" for the rest of his career. John McEnroe's parents never had that kind of success. If you find something that works, please send me an e-mail. In any case, Good Luck!

High School Tennis

High school tennis comes in many shapes and sizes: schools with great players, schools with clueless players, and everything in between. Some play in the spring, some play in the fall. I don't have much to say on the subject except to recommend that you find out what kind of program your school has and act accordingly. Your kid should not be intimidated if he/she isn't a great player. The rest of them may not be so good either, but if they are, it should at least be good practice. Don't expect too much from the tennis coach: pre-season practices are few, lots of matches in a short period of time, and often, no great knowledge of the sport or how to teach it.

For those who are competing for one of the singles spots, I always thought it unfair not to have challenge matches. I realize that court time may be limited, but each kid should have a chance to earn or defend a spot on the team. The match doesn't have to be best of three sets, it could be one set, or an extended tiebreak, but at least have something.

In many areas 7th and 8th graders can now play high school sports. If your child is good enough, he/she may want to play on the high school team. Tennis excellence is not the issue. The question should be: "Do I want my 7th grader practicing and traveling with juniors and seniors?" I don't know the answer, but at least you now have the question.

Summer Recreation programs

Most municipalities have some form of summer recreational programs for tennis. The cost is usually quite affordable, but the quality of the program is all over the map; some programs are run very professionally by competent instructors but most are run by high school or recently graduated high school students with one small hopper of balls, twenty students, and little or no motivation to get something accomplished. The only way to distinguish between the programs is to ask a few questions (How many instructors? How many students?), ask other parents, or show up and watch. *I warn you, it may not be pretty.*

Kids say the darnedest things

When I asked my ten year old student "Why did you miss that last shot?' I was hoping for a reasoned response along the line of "My racquet face was too open" or "My backswing was too big."

The reasoned response I got was "Because I'm a Bozo?"

Before the serve, I asked my bright teenaged student whether this serve was going out wide or down the middle. Never one to be boxed into a corner he simply replied that he would let the ball decide! And he did.

Bonus Chapter

Snow White
and the Seven Dwarfs

Why They Can't Win the Big Matches and
The Lessons You Can Learn from Them

Available now at
www.tennisfortherestofus.com

CENTER OF REASONABLE RETURNS (CRR)

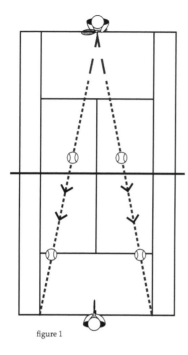

figure 1

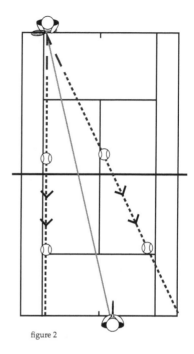

figure 2

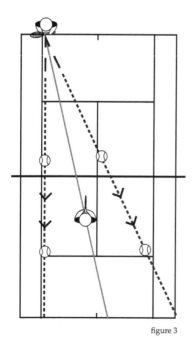

figure 3

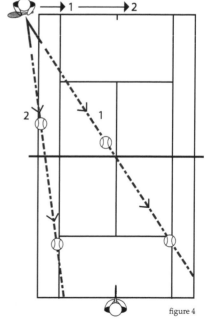

figure 4

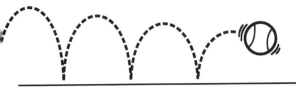

Chapter 25
Singles

Singles can be a little daunting because the correct strategy is not particularly obvious. "Hit it so hard they can't return it" or "Hit it where they ain't" is probably all that comes to mind, and you may not feel confident in your ability to do either of those. Fear not! I am going to explain singles in two simple concepts, though after I tell you what they are, you will likely exclaim "What the heck is he talking about?"

Concept #1. Place yourself in the Center of Reasonable Returns (CRR hereafter). *"What the heck is he talking about?"* Imagine you have hit the ball deep to the center of the court, and your opponent is standing in the center of the baseline returning it. Where is she likely to hit the ball. Figure 1 shows the range of likely shots. You should bisect the angle formed by those two lines. *"You told me there wouldn't be any math! Angle bisecting is geometry. I'm pretty sure that's math. Heck, that's even worse than math!"* This puts you right in the center of your baseline. Now imagine that you hit the ball to his forehand corner. What is a reasonable shot from this spot on the court? Straight down the line is one possibility and crosscourt to the corner of the service box is another (figure 2). Any angle sharper than that is either unrealistic or too good for me to worry about. The angle is bisected when you place yourself on the opposite side of the centerline from the shot you just hit, likewise if you had hit the ball to the opposite corner. How far from the center? It depends. If your opponent moves six feet, you move one. If he moves 12 feet, you move two feet. That's the **center of reasonable returns** from the baseline.

When you come into the net, the concept remains the same. You still want to be in the **center of reasonable returns,** and you bisect the angle exactly the same way, but a peculiar thing happens. When you draw that line and place yourself halfway between the net and the service line, the spot you should be standing on is not on the opposite side of the center line, but it's on the same side of the centerline (figure 3) "How can that be?" Geometry doesn't lie!

> When asked "Where should you stand and why ?" after watching a shot go into the corner, most players will not be able to answer both questions correctly. If the "where" is correct, the "Why?" is almost always "They are most likely to hit the ball crosscourt." Even if you were likely to hit the ball crosscourt, wouldn't you change your shot if your opponent was consistently too far to that side? I know that I would.

Concept #2: There are only two types of shots in tennis: *Attempted winners* and shots that will keep me in the point long enough to attempt a winner. Hopefully, some of the second type will cause him to miss, but maybe not. If your opponent is out of position or if he has hit a ball that allows you to hit it hard enough and far enough away from him, you should attempt to hit a winner. If he has not done that, you need to hit shots that will let you stay in the point until he does.

Attempting winners, even with a good shot, does not always mean *hitting* winners. Sometimes, your best shots are returned, and you have to start over.

Staying in position means staying in the Center of Reasonable Returns (CRR.) If you are hitting from a wide position, a "down-the-line" shot requires two more steps than a "crosscourt" shot to get to the CRR (opposite side of the center line.) Down the line shots from a wide position should be an attempted winner. Cross court shots should allow you to get back in position for the next shot. A hard shot is not always preferred. The more time you need to get back to the CRR, the higher and thus slower your shot should be (figure 4).

If the ball is closer to the middle of the court and recovery is easy, probe your opponent to find weaknesses.

If the ball is short and you are on your way to the net, remember that a crosscourt shot on your way to the net will take two more steps to get to the **CRR** than a down-the-line shot. From the middle of the court, I would hit to his weaker side and follow the ball.

Depth is Important: The deeper your shot lands in your opponent's court, the faster the ball will get to him and the more difficult it will be to return. Nothing slows a shot down more than the friction of hitting the ground. A ball that hits the service line and bounces to the baseline will be much slower and easier to return than a ball that hits closer to the baseline, even if both are hit with the same velocity.

- Deep shots keep your opponent from coming to the net and pressuring you.
- Deep shots by you create short shots by your opponent.
- Your opponent has less time to react when you hit from inside the court.
- Angled shots are easier to hit from inside the baseline.
- *Depth is Important!*

Singles is about keeping the ball in play until you can hit a winner or until your opponent misses.

- Hitting crosscourt, especially replying to wide shots, will make it easier for you to maintain good court position (CRR).
- Approach the net with a "down-the-line" shot to gain good net position. Vary this only if they are out of position or one ground stroke is significantly weaker than the other.
- *__Depth is important.__*
- Learn what you can from each point, then move on.

Tennis is usually a game of errors rather than a game of winners. The winner is most often the person who makes the fewest errors. Aiming for the lines, hitting the ball harder than is appropriate for the shot and your skill or trying too many "touch" shots are just some of the ways to lose the day. Keeping the ball in play forces your opponent to hit a winner before he misses, not just keep it in play until you do something stupid.

Successfully keeping the ball in play means hitting each shot well enough for your skill level. For example, if you are both beginners, getting the ball over the net and in the court anywhere will eventually earn you a victory. At the 3.0 level, hitting it with a little pace and a little depth is required. At the 4.0 level, more depth, pace, and spin are necessary to keep you in the point.

Common Tennis Terms you Need to Know

Anticipation – Guessing that succeeds. What most commentators describe as great *anticipation* is usually good positioning and great reaction. Net players who make incredible volleys are often touted to have "anticipated" the direction of the passing shot, but on closer inspection of the replay appear to have moved "after" the ball was struck.

Ideal Volley Position (IVP) – Halfway between the net and the service line.

Center of Reasonable Returns (CRR) – Midpoint of likely shots by your opponent. This is not necessarily the middle of the court. (See Singles)

Area of Responsibility – That part of the doubles court which each partner is theoretically responsible for. This does not mean that you must hit all the balls in your area. If your partner is in better position for the shot, he should take it.

Australian Formation – A doubles formation where the server stands close to the center line and the server's partner is at the net, but on the same side as the server, also close to the center line. This forces the opponent to change his returns from crosscourt to down the line. The benefits of this are explained in "Doubles".

Poaching – If the net player in doubles moves laterally in anticipation of a cross court return he is said to be poaching. Poaching is not moving to cut off a ball after it is hit. That is called "good doubles".

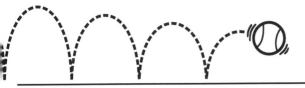

Chapter 26
Doubles

Doubles isn't the best tennis game, it's the best game, period.
Tony Trabert

You have two obligations in Doubles and no more:

1) Play as hard as you can
2) Win and lose as a team

That's it. If you told your partner you used to play on the Pro Circuit in Italy and you are only a 3.0 player, you might have some explaining to do, but other than that, no apologies are necessary. No "I'm sorry!" "My fault!" "It was my fault that we lost!" Conversely, don't roll your eyes when she misses an easy sitter at the net. Don't drop your racquet in disgust when he double faults on game point. When your partner is struggling, don't go silent on him or let him go silent on you. You are unlikely to win if your partner plays badly; encourage him to help him play his best.

The strategy of doubles is different from that of singles. A singles court is 78' x 27'. A doubles court is 78' x 36'. You get a whole 'nother player and they only make the court 9' wider. How cool is that? Way cool! And it makes for a very different game.

If all four players stayed on the baseline, very few winners would ever be hit. With only half a court to cover and plenty of time to react, most players can get to every ball. The same is true for the team on the other side. The occasional unforced error would be the only way to end a point. Boring!

CENTER OF REASONABLE RETURNS (CRR)

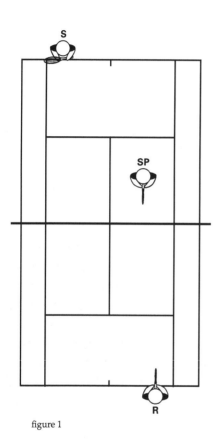

figure 1

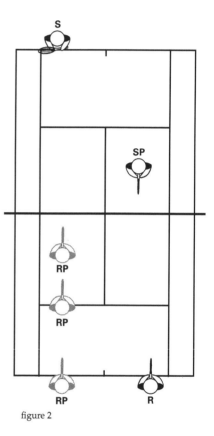

figure 2

Principles of Doubles

1) The Doubles court is divided left and right, not up and back.

(Figure 1) shows the typical positions for the server (S), server's partner (SP) and receiver (R). The server typically serves from the center of her area of responsibility, i.e. halfway between the center line and the outside doubles line. The receiver stands along the baseline (closer for a weak server, further back for a hard server) in the middle of likely serves. The server's partner is in the ideal volley position in the middle of his area of responsibility.

2) Net players can hit winners.

Baseliners keep the ball in play and occasionally force an error. If this is true, and it is, shouldn't you try to get to the net to hit winners? Yes, you should. How do I do that?

3) You must earn your way to the net to be successful there.

The server's partner starts at the net under the assumption that the server has an advantage against the receiver. A good serve will make it difficult for the returner to keep the ball away from the net player. The server may also follow a strong serve to the net (serve and volley tactic) hoping for a weak return. In doubles, it is easier to be successful at the net because you have less court to cover than in singles. Clean passing shots are much harder to hit in doubles. Other ways to get to the net include moving in after a short ball, moving in after a strong return of serve, and lobbing over your opponents' heads and taking the net as they retreat backwards. Hitting an easy ball crosscourt and running in may not be earning our way to the net. Unless you make your opponent uncomfortable with your shot, he is likely to make life miserable for you by either hitting the perfect lob, driving the ball to your feet, or hitting that clean passing shot.

4) Opponents at the net make excellent targets for net players with easy shots.

A net player with an easy ball can hit it hard into the "area" of the opposing net player. Since the ball is fast and the distance between them is short, the opposing net player has a very hard time returning this shot, if he can reach it. This same shot hit to the baseliner takes more time to arrive, allowing more time to prepare for the shot. If you cannot attack the net player, keep it away from him, for you also can make an "excellent target."

Let's go back to our Doubles Diagram (figure 1). Where is the receiver's partner (RP)? Remember that we must earn our way to the net. Figure 2 shows three positions for the receiver's partner.

Remember that we must earn our way to the net. Figure 2 shows three positions for the receiver's partner.

The baseline position is used when there is little confidence that the receiver can make a good return of serve. This does not necessarily mean "he has no confidence in me!" It might mean you are facing a good server. Since the net player, or the server moving in, may get an easy shot, why be an "excellent target?" Give yourself every opportunity to get into the point by giving yourself as much time as possible to react to the shot.

The service line position is used when we can reasonably assume, but are not certain, that the receiver can make a good return. If he does, we can move into the ideal volley position (IVP) and perhaps hit a winning volley ourselves. If not, we have some time to react to the shot. We also help cover the diagonal shot of the net player into an open part of the court.

The third position is at the IVP, knowing that our partner can keep the ball away from the net player and we can be in perfect position to hit a winning volley ourselves. If our partner cannot keep the ball away from the net player, we will lose this point. Usually, we don't have this much confidence.

Offense, Defense, Neutral
Every point at every stage is in one of the three categories above. In the beginning, the point should be neutral. If the server has a big serve, they may assume they are going to start on the offensive, just as you may assume you will be starting on the defensive, and everyone will position themselves accordingly.

If the serve is moderate, we may take a more neutral position, and if

NEUTRAL

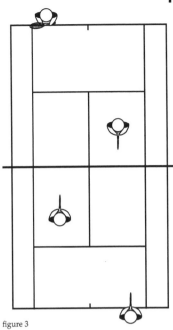

figure 3

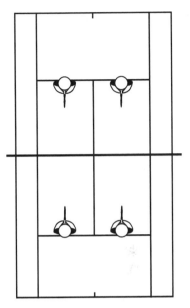

figure 4

OFFENSE TO DEFENSE

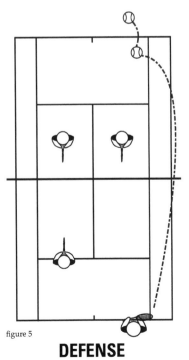

figure 5

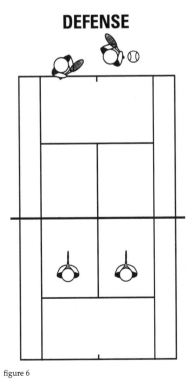

figure 6

DEFENSE TO OFFENSE

it is weak, the receivers may assume the offensive.

The first two diagrams show a neutral position. Both teams with one up and one back (figure 3), the second with all four players at the net (figure 4). A neutral position changes into an offensive position when one team has both players at the net (figure 5) and can change again when those same net players are forced back to the baseline by a good lob (figure 6).

Once the ball is in play, certain concepts apply:
1) If it's good for one, it's good for both. If it's bad for one, it's bad for both. If you hit a good shot and move forward, your partner will not move backwards. If you are chasing a good lob, your partner will not run to the net.

2) If we are on the offensive, we tend to move forward. If we are on the defensive, we move back or hold our position. On the offensive, we would move from the service line to the IVP; from the baseline we would move to the service line or the IVP if we could get there in one shot. On the defensive, you would move from the IVP to the service line, or in the case of a high, but short lob, all the way to the baseline.

3) A baseliner, crosscourt from the shot just hit, moves in the **opposite** direction from the netplayer. Figure 7 shows how much of the court is covered by the net player. Baseliner moves right to cover the remaining court.

4) Net players move with the ball (figure 8). If both players are at the net, they would move left and right together in the same direction as the shot they just hit. Figure 7 shows how both net players moving with the ball covers shot 1, down the middle. They also cover shot 2, down the line. They don't cover shot 3, a sharp crosscourt angle over the high part of the net with little room on the other side. If you have to give up something, this is it.

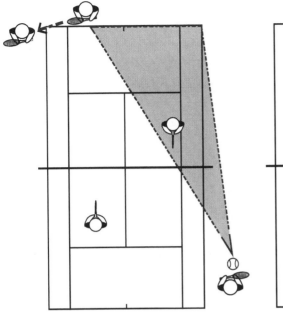

figure 7

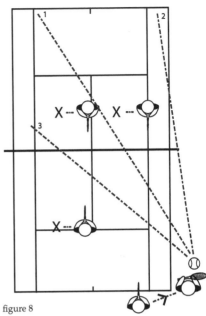

figure 8

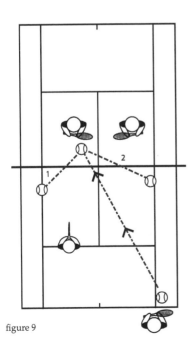

figure 9

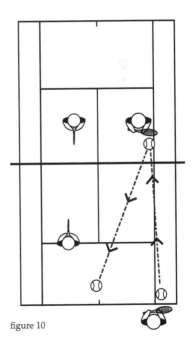

figure 10

Doubles Philosophy

1) Do not hit to the net player when a winner is not likely. The baseliner is unlikely to hit a winner, net players often do.

2) When hitting from the baseline to two net players, hitting cross-court or down the middle does not create winning angles for the net players, down the line shots do (figures 9 and 10).

3) It is difficult to hit a winner past two well-positioned net players. Do not be afraid to hit the ball at them. No, I didn't say "Hit them!" If only a weak shot is possible, you must lob.

4) At the net, plan on hitting the ball back to the baseliner, unless, you have a better idea. A better idea is an easy ball with which to attack the net player. It is much easier to think your way through an easy ball than to think of what to do with a tough ball, therefore, back to the baseliner unless you can think of something better.

5) Easy overheads should attack the area of the person closest to the net or an unguarded portion of the court.

6) Lobs hit over the heads of the net players allow the lobbers to move into the net. Feel free to do so.

7) Communicate with your partner during the point. Do not conduct a dialogue. "Yours!" "Mine!" "Back up!" "Look out!" and similar statements work a lot better than "Is that mine?" or "Yours?" What if that answer is "No?"

8) The best reply to a good overhead is another lob. Groundstrokes hit after overheads are not as easy as they seem. If the overhead is weak, a groundstroke is fine.

9) Make adjustments. If returning serve is a problem, move the receiver's partner to the baseline, don't try to hit so hard, or lob the return.

10) If the other team is lobbing successfully, perhaps the net players should move back a step.

Advanced Doubles Philosophy

It's nice to know where everyone is on the court so you can plan your shots accordingly. "I've got a tough service return, better keep it away from the net player." What if you don't know where the net player is? Service returns just got tougher. **Poaching** is when the server's partner, in anticipation of a crosscourt return moves before the service return is hit (figure 11). When timed well, it is hard for the receiver, who has enough to do just dealing with the serve, to be sure where the net player is. A signal from the net player to the server, usually an open hand behind the back, alerts the server who must cover the side recently vacated by his partner. Server's partner moving after the ball is hit is not poaching. It's just good doubles for a net player to move and cut off the shot.

If consistent crosscourt returns are a problem and poaching is not the solution, why not try the **Australian formation**? Is that where you put all the Sheilas up close to the net and let the Blokes play tennis? Not quite, mate. The Australian formation puts the server's partner on the same side of the court as the server (figure 12) to force the receiver to hit the ball somewhere other than crosscourt. The server stands close to the center line and then moves to the openside of the court after the serve. The advantages of "going Australian" include forcing the receiver to do something different from what was successful and it may also cover up a weak side or force them to hit to your stronger side. Example: By going Australian when serving from the Ad court, a right-handed server would move right after serving and probably get a forehand. If the team plays conventionally, the server's next shot will likely be a backhand. If your backhand stinks, that could be a problem.

As with so many things, familiarity breeds contempt. Overuse of the Australian formation will force the other team to adapt. Eventually they will stop scratching their heads and start to figure out what to do. When they do, your bag of tricks will be empty. My advice is to save it for the occasional important point and keep them guessing.

POACHING   AUSTRALIAN FORMATION

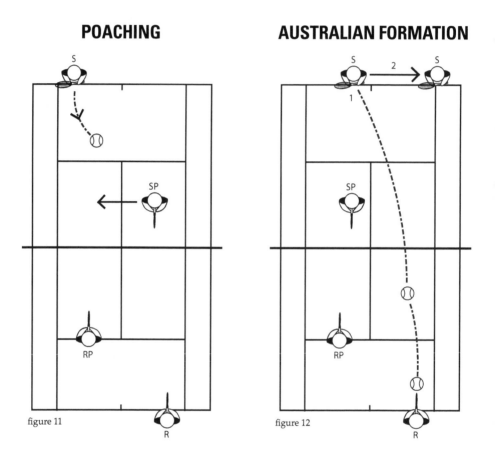

figure 11   figure 12

WARNING: Some teams never poach, other teams just love it. For those who never poach, try it once in a while. For those who love it, note that poaching too much is as predictable as never poaching, and you may also notice that volleying on the move is not as easy as it looks.

128

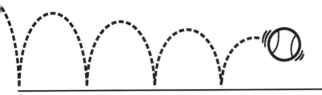

Chapter 27

Mixed Doubles

Whenever possible, hit it at the girl.
Bill Tilden

I cannot improve upon the strategy of the greatest player of the first fifty years of tennis.

Serious mixed doubles strategy can be summed up by Tilden's quote, but so much of mixed doubles is not serious tennis, but social tennis.

Mixed doubles is fraught with peril for the guys. Make no mistake about it, social mixed doubles often tests a relationship in ways that few activities can. The rules below are just the tip of the iceberg and have general applications. You still don't know your unique "Couples" dynamic. Don't say you haven't been warned.

The rules for social tennis are a little different than for tournament play.

Rule #1. If you are a guy, do not hit the opposing woman, nor put her in fear of her life every time you get an easy ball. Hitting a 100 mph overhead at someone 20 feet away and just missing isn't a whole lot more pleasant for her than being plunked in the back occasionally.

Rule #2. If you are a guy, don't hit your partner with your "BIG" serve. Did I say "don't?" I meant to say "NEVER"! Nothing shouts "long drive home" more than a wife or girlfriend with "Penn 3" tattooed to her back

bad   worse

By the way, if you have serves with names, like **"Big Boy"** and **"Sneaky Pete,"** I'm not sure I can be of any assistance to you!

Rule #3. The better partner, be it male or female, should not give the partner *"the LOOK"* when they miss an easy shot. Ladies, you know what I'm talkin' 'bout. As the undisputed masters of *"the LOOK,"* save it for a more appropriate time than when your not-so-good tennis playing spouse has kindly agreed to be dragged out onto the court and humiliated so that he doesn't have to hear "We never do anything together anymore."

Rule #4. Mixed doubles is often played with 4.0 men and 3.0 women or other equally wide skill disparities. The men want to be nice. The women can smell condescension a mile away. What to do, what to do????

OK guys, let's think this through. You have a 90 mph first serve but she can't return anything over 60 mph. Don't serve it at 20 mph, she'll hate you; serve it at 60 or 70 mph. She will feel good about her returns when she does hit it back and you can get the condescension monkey off your back.

The second problem is that a 4.0 man can usually hit a winner off anything a 3.0 woman hits to him. I have seen guys whack winners left and right over-powering the woman and the man, bringing them an early case of tennis elbow. When I suggest that this was not the most fun way to spend a Saturday evening, they stop hitting the ball so hard. Unfortunately, they now resort to clever placements and drop shots that the woman cannot get a racquet on. This is just as frustrating as being overpowered. Just because you can hit a winner, doesn't mean you have to. Why not challenge the weaker player by hitting a shot that she may be able to handle, but not necessarily. Most points will be lost eventually by the weaker player but the rallies will be longer; the lesser players will have hit some winners and a good time will be had by all.

You might even have some conversation on the ride home.

An athletic, happily married couple decided to play in a mixed doubles tournament. They were not great tennis players, both 3.0, but she was a very athletic ex-dancer and he was a big time hockey player. They were up 3-1 in the first set when it happened. They were both at the net when a short, floaty ball came to her. She backed up to take it on the bounce while he moved in to crush it in the air, which he did. That was it. They lost 6-3, 6-0. She later explained that it was at that moment that "I realized that he didn't respect my game." His summation was a little more to the point: "We played the first four games as partners and the rest as husband and wife!" I tell you fellas, "Mixed Doubles is fraught with peril!"

Worst post-match handshake conversation ever

After a 6-1, 6-0 drubbing the loser shook hands and said "Nice Match."
The winner replied, "I can't believe I played so bad!"

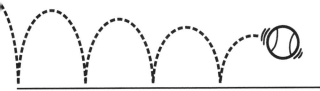

Chapter 28

Thoughts On Match Play

Every time you win, it diminishes the fear a little bit.
You never really cancel the fear of losing. You just keep challenging it.
Arthur Ashe

Even though you are the only one you care about out there, tennis matches are not just about you. It is about *you and your **opponent.*** Only loved ones ask, "Did you play well?" as their first question. Everyone else asks "Who won?"

"So what's your point?"

My point is, tennis matches are not necessarily about playing well; they are about winning and losing and while playing well should help you win, winning *"ugly"* is OK, too. Ultimately, you are measured by your wins and losses.

General thoughts on match play:

• You should know your strengths and weaknesses (I know you think you have no strengths and lots of weaknesses, or vice versa for the guys, but don't be so hard on yourself) and form a game plan accordingly. For instance, if you are shaky from the baseline and are more confident at the net, try to come in every chance you get.

• Evaluate your opponent during the warm-up. Is her forehand strong and her backhand weak? Did he look shaky on his warm-up volleys? The warm-up serves should give you a clue as to what you'll be up against. The serves may be fast, but do they go in often, particularly under pressure? What is the second serve like?

- Play *your* game, at least for awhile. One great backhand service return doesn't mean he's got a great backhand service return. We all get lucky. Maybe he got lucky on his first two and won't hit another one in 'til Labor Day.

- In the course of "playing your game" you will find out what she likes and doesn't like. Make some adjustments if necessary. If you are winning, these adjustments will probably be minor. If losing, you may have to rethink quite a bit.

- If you find something that works, use it, but don't overdo it. Hitting high, loopy balls may drive her crazy, but if that's all you've done for a set and a half and she figures out how to handle it, what will you do next? It is better to use this strategy as often as necessary, but not exclusively. It is very comforting to know how to win a point when you need one. Don't give that away by giving her lots of opportunities to figure out a counter strategy. In doubles, this applies to poaching, unusual formations and/or excessive lobbing.

> I didn't have the same fitness or ability as the other girls,
> so I had to beat them with my mind.
> **Martina Hingis**

- Don't mistake *"poor execution"* with a poor game plan. If you keep missing easy volleys when you come to the net, it doesn't mean your strategy is wrong, it means that so far today, you are a lousy volleyer. If you don't think that will continue, don't change your plan.

- The match is about winning and losing, not about losing by a *"respectable"* score. If you've just lost the first set 6-2 and you realize against this formidable opponent you need to hit the ball harder and deeper, then try to hit harder and deeper. Who knows, you might just pull it off. If not, and you lose 6-0, what have you lost?

You would have lost with your initial strategy and you lost switching game plans. It's seems the same to me. Either way, chalk up one loss. Tomorrow is another day.

• It is more important to **control the momentum of the match** than it is to be ahead in the score. If it hasn't happened to you yet, it will; you are ahead 6-0, 3-0, cruising along, when suddenly things start to change. You may let down a little bit. He may start to play better. Maybe the judgmental spouse or parent decided to leave. Maybe his back finally loosened up. Who can say why, but things are changing and they are changing fast; and before you know it, what seemed like an easy win has turned into an embarrassing loss. It has happened to us all. If things are going well, don't get too excited, something might change. If things are going badly, don't get too down on yourself; hey, something might change. *Play one point at a time.*

• We should learn something from every match. We probably learn more from the losses than the wins, and I guess that is some small consolation.

> People don't seem to understand it's a damn war out there.
> **Jimmy Connors**

• **Enjoy the Struggle.** Let me repeat that. **Enjoy the Struggle.** Winning isn't fun if you already know the outcome, a fact that becomes all too obvious when you realize from the warm-up that this guy is not very good. Losing isn't any fun either, if you know you are going to lose. Ah, but when the outcome is in doubt, and you have to come up with good shots in pressure situations, that's when the game is at its best. Win or lose, this is what it's all about. **Have fun!**

> I think that's why I'm playing so well – I'm enjoying myself.
> **Kim Clijsters**

At that point it was just very flowing, I didn't even think about it.
I just went on court and did my thing and was very happy about it.
Martina Hingis

But sometimes you just don't do well.
Martina Hingis

The older you get, the more you learn.
Martina Hingis

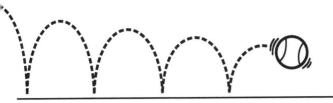

Chapter 29

The Rules of Tennis

The tennis court is 78' long x 27' wide, 36' wide for doubles. The net is 42" at the sides and 36" in the middle.

Rule 1. The right to serve, receive, choose your side, or give the opponent these choices is decided by a toss of a coin or racquet. If the choice of service or receiver is chosen, the opponent chooses which side to start, or vice versa.

Rule 2. Opponents stand on opposite sides of the court. The player who delivers the ball to start the point is called the server. The player who stands opposite and crosscourt from the server is the receiver.

Rule 3. The server shall stand behind the baseline on the right side (deuce court) within the boundaries of the singles court when playing singles and within the doubles sideline when playing doubles. All even points are played from the deuce court and odd number points played from the left side (ad- vantage court.) The server shall not serve until the receiver is ready. Serves are made diagonally, from the deuce court to the opponent's service box on the deuce court: Advantage court to advantage box. If the server misses his target twice, he loses the point. If the ball hits the net and goes in the correct service box, another serve is granted. If the server steps on or over the baseline before contact is made, the serve is deemed a fault.

Rule 4. The receiver can stand where he likes but must let the ball bounce in the service box. If the ball does not land in the service box, it is deemed a fault and a second serve is given. If the ball is hit before the ball bounces, the server wins the point.

Rule 5. Love means zero in tennis. The first point is 15. The second point is 30. The third is 40 and the fourth is game. The server always calls his score first. If the server wins the first point, the score is 15-love. If he loses, it is love-15. Love means zero in tennis If the score is 40-40, also known as deuce, one side must win by two points. Advantage-In means if the server wins the next point, he wins the game. Advantage-Out means the receiver has a chance to win the game on the next point.

LOVE 15-30-40 –GAME

Rule 6. Serve alternates after each game. The first to win 6 games, by two, wins the set. The first to win 2 sets wins the match. If the score is 6-6, a tie-breaker is played. This is scored by ones. The first team to score 7 points winning by two wins the set. The tiebreaker continues until one side wins by two. Hence, Game-Set-Match.

Rule 7. If the ball goes into the net or outside the boundaries of the court, the player who hit that ball loses the point. If the ball hits the net during the point and goes into the opponent's court, the ball is in play. If the ball is hit out of play, the hitter loses the point. A player loses the point if he touches the net, throws his racquet to hit the ball, bounces the ball over the net, hits a part of the surroundings such as the roof, or a tree, or if the ball touches him or his partner or she deliberately tries to distract the opponent.

Rule 8. A let is called during the point if a ball rolls on the court or there is a distraction from someone besides the players on the court.

Rule 9. A ball that lands on the line is good. When unsure if the ball is good, the benefit of the doubt MUST go to the opponent.

Rule 10. If players serve out of turn or serve to the wrong person or court, the point or game will stand and order will be resumed following the point or game.

Coming Soon
(hopefully by Christmas 2008)

Tennis
For the Rest of Us
Part Two

Ok, so now I'm hooked.
How do I get good?

If you didn't like this book, you won't like the next one either, but if you did, go to www.tennisfortherestofus.com for an update.

While you're there, please leave a comment on this book.

I know you liked it Mom, let someone else use the website.
It might crash with more than one user.

22530205R00081